DOES GOD EXIST?

DOES GOD EXIST?

Science says 'yes!'

ALAN HAYWARD

Marshall Morgan & Scott

To that small band of courageous biologists who have dared to say publicly what many others know in their hearts – that their emperor has nothing on.

Lakeland Paperbacks
Marshall Morgan & Scott
3 Beggarwood Lane, Basingstoke, Hants., UK.

Copyright © Alan Hayward 1978
This book first published as 'God Is' in a hardback edition in 1978, reprinted in 1979.
This paperback edition published in 1983.
ISBN 0 551 05585 5

Biblical quotations are from the Revised Standard Version copyrighted 1946 and 1952, © 1971 and 1973, by the Division of Christian Education of the National Council of the Churches of Christ in the USA, unless otherwise stated.

Printed and bound in Great Britain by
Cox & Wyman Ltd, Reading

CONTENTS

AUTHOR'S NOTE

I am extremely grateful to a number of people who have helped me with this book.

In particular I should like to thank Professor Sir Ernst Chain and Professor Gerald Kerkut, who, although they do not share my Christian faith, generously gave of their time to read the first draft and comment on it. My friends Robert Clark, Alan Fowler, Vernon Fowler, Ivan Stockley, John Wenham and Harry Whittaker, along with two members of my own family, also read the first draft and suggested so many valuable improvements that the reader must have nearly as much cause to be grateful to them as I have. I am also deeply indebted to Rita Dyson for her superb secretarial assistance.

Above all, I must acknowledge how much this book owes to my wife. It has been an exceptionally difficult book to write, and its production has put heavy burdens on us both; had she not helped me along the uphill stretches, I doubt whether I could have carried on to the end of the road.

ALAN HAYWARD

East Kilbride
October 1977

PREFACE

Perhaps it is obvious to you that God exists. If so, that's fine; that is how it ought to be. Read no further. You do not need this book.

Instead, try lending it to your friends, because some of them are in great need of its message. You can be sure of that in these days of increasing unbelief.

Perhaps you have an open mind on the subject, and would like to see some evidence that God exists, but are daunted by the size of this book. Then try dipping into any chapter from 4 onwards – that is where the real meat of the book lies.

If you happen to have strong objections to believing, or have a feeling that belief is somehow old-fashioned or unscientific, be sure to start at chapter 1. The first three chapters will be of especial interest to you.

Chapter 1

A MYTH THAT NEEDS
EXPLODING

Some years ago I attended a scientific conference behind the Iron Curtain. After each day's work was done the other British delegates went off together for a night on the town. But I excused myself from their company, saying that I had other plans. I wanted to see for myself how Christianity was surviving under communist rule.

To my delight I found that it was faring very well. 'Of course we are harassed by the authorities,' the leader of one evangelical group told me. 'But despite that our numbers show a steady increase every year.

'We don't have any scientists among our members, though. In fact we look upon you as a bit of a freak. How do you manage to reconcile your Christian faith with your scientific training?'

I smiled. 'Somebody has been having you on. I could name at least a hundred of my friends and colleagues who are both well-qualified scientists and committed Christians. In Britain there are just as many scientists who are believers as there are in any other profession.'

He was astonished at this, and seemed to find it hard to believe. In his country the schools teach that 'science has shown there is no God'. Unless a student accepts this proposition he is unlikely to qualify as a scientist, and so it is not surprising that scientists who believe in God are not very numerous in Eastern Europe.

What is surprising is the way in which many people in the West have adopted a similar view. In fact, you might almost say that the tale of science's victory over religion is the greatest myth of our time. It runs like this:

Long, long ago men were terribly ignorant. In those

days everybody believed in God, or gods. They were not to be blamed for this: it was the only way these primitive men could explain the things they did not understand.

Nowadays there is no excuse for such ignorance, since science has solved the riddle of the universe. We know now that it wasn't formed by a Creator – it evolved by natural forces. Only children, old dodderers and ignoramuses believe in God today.

The facts behind the myth

The first thing wrong with that account is the way it misrepresents the past. In primitive times a belief in the supernatural was by no means universal. Wherever men thought deeply about the mysteries of life there were two schools of thought.

Among the ancient Greeks, for example, there were philosophers like Plato who believed in the Greek gods, and philosophers like Protagoras who did not.

Even earlier, in the nation of Israel there were men who pondered the origin of the universe. Many of them agreed with their hymn-writer, who sang:

The heavens are telling the glory of God
And the firmament proclaims his handiwork.[1]

Thou didst knit me together in my mother's womb ...
Wonderful are thy works![2]

This, they thought, was only common sense. Look up at the sky, down at the flowers beneath your feet, around you at the distant landscape. Examine that superb machine, your own body. All the marvels of nature testify to the existence of a Creator. How else could such things have come into being?

Many of the Jews of thirty centuries ago felt like that, but not all. There were some who took another line, one that is very familiar to us today: 'Rubbish! I want better proof than that before I can believe in God.'

We know of these men's existence because other Old Testament passages refer to them like this:

> The fool says in his heart,
> 'There is no God.'[3]

The controversy must have gone on for centuries. It was still continuing when the New Testament was being written by men like the apostle Paul, who used the same basic arguments: 'Ever since the creation of the world his (God's) invisible nature . . . has been clearly perceived in the things that have been made',[4] and 'He (God) did not leave himself without witness, for he did good and gave you from heaven rains and fruitful seasons'.[5] When Paul spoke like that his hearers soon divided into two camps. Some agreed that he sounded very reasonable; others told him he must be joking.[6]

So there is nothing new about a world in which some people believe in a Creator and others do not.

The world's greatest scientist

A few years ago an American scientist was asked on a radio programme, 'Who in your opinion was the greatest scientist who ever lived?'

He replied: 'There is no problem. I feel that most historians of science would declare at once that Isaac Newton was the greatest scientific mind the world has seen.'[7]

This intellectual giant made it quite plain where he stood. In the most famous of all his books, Newton explained mathematically why the solar system behaves as it does. Then, in conclusion, he declared: 'This most beautiful system of the sun, planets and comets, could only proceed from the counsel and dominion of an intelligent and powerful Being.'[8]

As always, there was another point of view. Some of Newton's scientific colleagues were atheists. Not very many of them, but enough to worry him and provoke him into writing an essay on atheism, in which he said: 'Atheism is so senseless and odious to mankind that it never had many professors.'

He went on to write about the way the human body is constructed, and especially the eye, with which some of his own research was closely connected. At intervals he asked such questions as, 'Can it be by accident that ...', and, 'Did blind chance know that ...', and he ended with the bold assertion 'These and such like considerations always have and ever will prevail with mankind, to believe that there is a Being who made all things ...'[9]

Scientists today

Present-day unbelievers are cock-a-hoop. Newton was evidently wrong when he thought that belief in God 'ever would prevail with mankind', since unbelievers can now outvote believers any time they like.

One unbelieving scientist, Sir Julian Huxley, enjoyed crowing over the rising tide of atheism: 'The supernatural is being swept out of the universe ... God is beginning to resemble not a ruler, but the last fading smile of a cosmic Cheshire cat.'[10]

But Huxley's jubilation was not only premature, it was downright misleading. They may be fewer than they used to be, but there are still quite a number of eminent twentieth-century scientists who echo Newton's views. Even Einstein, the nearest equivalent to a Newton that our century can provide, wrote:

A knowledge of the existence of something we cannot penetrate, of *the manifestations of the profoundest reason* and the most radiant beauty, which are only accessible to our reason in their most elementary forms – it is this knowledge and this emotion that constitute the truly religious attitude; in this sense, and in this alone, *I am a deeply religious man.*[11] (My italics)

14

Einstein may not have shared Newton's belief in the God of the Bible. But evidently he agreed with Newton that there must be some sort of supremely wise Being at the back of nature.

Shortly before he died, Jung, who was then regarded as the greatest living psychologist, was asked by a television interviewer, 'Do you believe in God?' Millions of viewers heard him reply, 'I do not need to *believe* in His existence, I *know*![12]

Time after time within the past few years the late Dr Wernher von Braun, who for many years was America's top space-scientist, made similar declarations in public. He repeatedly used the same argument as Newton – that creation implies a Creator – which he regarded as being just as scientifically sound in the 1970s as it was in the 1670s.

Men like von Braun are not isolated exceptions. Many scientists today are committed Christians. For example, there is a British society called the Research Scientists Christian Fellowship, and it has about seven hundred members,[13] yet only a small minority of the Christian research scientists that I know belong to it. If a full count of British research scientists who firmly believe in God were made, it would certainly run into thousands – perhaps many thousands.

Yet despite these facts, as a recent article in *New Scientist* said:

The lay view persists – of scientists having 'disproved' religion. It is a view that commonly expects scientists to be nonbelievers; that Darwin put the last nails in God's coffin; and that a succession of scientific and technological innovations since have ruled out the possibility of any resurrection. *It is a view that is wildly wrong* ... a straw poll among universities, research establishments, and industrial laboratories indicates that as many as *eight out of every ten scientists follow a religious faith* or countenance principles that are 'non-scientific'.[14] (My italics)

15

Even though that writer's figure of 8 out of 10 may well be an overestimate, his main point is undeniably true: an astonishing number of scientists today believe in God.

Still an open question

What would Newton think if he were to come back to life today? Would he now side with Huxley, and say, 'If only I had known what later science was going to discover, I should never have spoken as I did'? Or would he stick to his guns, and line up alongside Einstein, Jung, von Braun, and all the other believing scientists of the twentieth century?

Obviously, we can only guess. But it would be exceedingly difficult to argue that Newton would have to change his mind. There has always been a good case for belief in God, and always some arguments you could use against it, too. That is why, in every age, there have been some believers and some unbelievers. And the fact is that modern science has hardly affected the balance of the arguments. True, it has provided some new reasons that can be used to justify unbelief – but it has also provided a great many new reasons for belief.

The net result is that the grounds for believing in God today are every bit as strong as they were in Newton's day. The purpose of this book is first to deal with the unbelievers' objections, and then to set out the case for belief in God. I shall aim to do it in language that the ordinary reader can understand.[15]

This will create a few problems. Homely, unscientific language may make for easy reading, but it is often slightly inaccurate when applied to scientific subjects. Never mind, that is a price we shall have to accept.

My apologies, then, to those scientist readers who find my loose terminology objectionable. I can offer them one crumb of consolation: the notes at the end of the book are for the benefit of people who want to dig deeper, and especially for those who are studying my case in an attempt to answer it, and so I shall be a little more particular about my language in the notes.

The notes, incidentally, are not at all essential for an understanding of the book itself. The ordinary reader will probably find the book more enjoyable if he ignores the notes altogether – at least on a first reading.

Chapter 2

THE HEART OF THE MATTER

In the middle of the last century Karl Marx was working on his world-shaking book, *Das Kapital*. He was determined to improve the miserable lot of the nineteenth-century working classes, and so he urged them to rise up and overthrow their masters.

Few of them took much notice of him. There was from Marx's point of view one great snag, in that, unlike Marx, most people believed in God. Religion acted like a drug, soothing the oppressed masses and making them content with their chains.

There was, thought Marx, only one thing for it: somehow the hold of religion would have to be broken. After that it would be a simple matter to overturn the unjust capitalist society. But how was he to achieve that first goal, and convince people there was no God?

While Marx wrestled with this problem he discovered an unexpected ally. A biologist called Charles Darwin had suddenly made the headlines with a startling new publication called *The Origin of Species*. Marx soon decided that this remarkable book would do his work for him. He was so convinced of this that he actually asked permission (which was refused) to dedicate *Das Kapital* to Charles Darwin.[1]

Marx was astonishingly farsighted about this, for time has proved his judgement to have been absolutely correct. In the century and a quarter since it appeared, the *Origin* has done more to change men's religious thinking than any book since the *Koran*.

Yet, curiously, a great many religious people are unaware of what Darwin's book has really done. They have adjusted their views of the Book of Genesis, so as to interpret 'God made man in his own image' to mean,

'God allowed man to be descended from a sort of ape.' Apart from this, they think that religious life can carry on as usual, just as if Darwin had never been born.

They could hardly be more wrong. As Marx's brilliant mind realised, the real issue is very much deeper than that.

Before Darwin, the believer always had one unbeatable card to play: 'Look at this wonderful world. If God didn't make it, how did it get here?' There was no answer.

Darwin and his successors changed all that. After *The Origin of Species*, theories followed thick and fast, explaining the origin of just about everything else. If you were the least bit trendy you soon accepted that human society just evolved; that religion just evolved; that the first spark of life on earth just evolved; that the solar system just evolved; as for the universe itself, well maybe that evolved, too, if we did but know.

Here at last was the answer to all the unbeliever's problems. 'Evolution' was the perfect explain-everything word. It was delightfully flexible: you could use it to describe processes you understood, and you could also use it to cover up your ignorance of anything you didn't understand.

So the believer found his ace trumped. Before he could get any further than, 'If God didn't make it . . .', the triumphant cry, 'Evolution did!' would cut him short.

Needless to say, the issue is far more complex than I have portrayed it. But the man in the street tends to see it in those simple terms.[2]

This is very loose thinking on his part, because there are a great many wonders in nature that the theory of evolution does not even pretend to explain. The evidence in chapter 4 alone, for example, is enough to make a powerful case for believing in God, and it has nothing to do with living things; it would still stand, even if Darwinism could be proved true.

But the average person is all too ready to brush aside

facts like that. To him, the theory of evolution provides a wonderful alternative to believing in a Creator. And he reacts accordingly. At the last Opinion Research Centre poll, in 1974, only 29 per cent of British people interviewed believed in God, compared with 38 per cent in 1963.[3]

If tombstones could talk, Marx's grave in Highgate cemetery would never stop chortling, 'I told you so!'

Keep a level head

As the whole philosophy of evolution is so crucial to the question of God's existence, we must obviously take a cool, calm and careful look at it.

Unfortunately, this is easier said than done. Evolution is one of those subjects like abortion, apartheid and capital punishment. Mention any of them in a crowded room and the temperature immediately rises a couple of degrees. It is extremely difficult to have a quiet, thoughtful look at a subject so heavily charged with emotion and prejudice.

Nevertheless, we must try. But before starting, let me doff my cap respectfully to three parties with whom I must politely disagree.

First, there is the if-evolution-is-good-enough-for-the-Archbishop-it's-good-enough-for-me school of thought. For people who have a great respect for Authority, this is a devastating argument. The majority of theologians – and an *overwhelming* majority of *eminent* theologians – have accepted evolution as proven fact. Consequently, it seems impertinent for any rank-and-file Christian to question it.

It might indeed be impertinent if it were not for one important fact. By and large, the theologians have accepted evolution a lot less critically than the scientists have. As we shall see later, many distinguished biologists have their reservations about various aspects of evolution, and some have questioned its very foundations.

That being so, it is rather strange to find evolution taken for granted in so many theological circles, including most university departments of theology and the religious department of the BBC.

An editorial in a leading scientific journal recently complained that scientists are very prone to jump on bandwagons.[4] Of course they are: it is a universal human failing. Eminent churchmen also suffer from it, just like the rest of us.

Unfortunately, their lack of scientific training prevents them realising that the evolutionary bandwagon is creaking and groaning a bit. So up they climb, and away they go, not caring that they have left behind the number one reason for belief in God. They never notice that the destination board on the bandwagon says UNBELIEF, and that its driver is an atheist, laughing his head off at the thought of all those well-meaning Christian passengers.

At the other end of the theological scale are the extreme fundamentalists. I have a great deal of sympathy for them; their heart is in the right place. And yet many believers like myself are deeply embarrassed by them, because of the arguments they use.

Often there are some very valuable points in their books, points that deserve serious consideration. But nobody except their own supporters takes much notice, because serious students are put off by the general air of unreality about this literature.

For example, one recent book, beautifully produced and widely circulated, solemnly assures its readers that dinosaurs did not become extinct until long after the Flood.[5] How did Noah pack those big beasts into the ark along with all the other animals? No problem. The writer explains that Noah would have been able to select a batch of baby dinosaurs to take on board!

There seems to be a great shortage of books written from a standpoint between these two extremes. That is why I have felt obliged to write this one.

Scientists too can be unreasonable

The third class of people with whom I must disagree are those scientists who say, 'No discussion, please. Evolution is a proven fact.'

To their shame, some biologists are constantly making statements like that – and the more eminent they are, the more extravagant their claims seem to be. Here are a couple of examples, picked almost at random from a whole stack on my desk:

> The first point to make about Darwin's theory is that it is no longer a theory, but a fact. – Sir Julian Huxley[6]

> Evolution is not, of course, only a theory, as some elderly, sheltered people may perhaps still imagine; it is as much a reality as are the facts of geography. – Sir Alister Hardy[7]

Those statements were aimed at the general public. When addressing their colleagues, scientists are sometimes even more emphatic. For instance, in 1972 an editorial in *Nature*, one of the world's foremost scientific journals, declared: 'Darwinism occupies a place in science at least as strong as Newton's Laws.[8]

I find it difficult to say anything more than, 'Phew!' The audacity of such a statement is breathtaking. Newton's Laws are so easy to verify by experiment that nearly every scientist has seen them demonstrated either at school or at university. They are almost as self-evident as the fact that running water always flows downhill. To compare them with Darwinism is like saying that you can show by scientific experiments, any time you like, that Darwinism is a fact.

Is that so? Hardly. The editor of *Nature* forgot one slightly embarrassing fact. Five years before he made that sweeping assertion, his own journal had published a paper in which a famous American biologist and his co-author said:

22

Our theory of evolution has become, as Popper[9] described, one which cannot be refuted by any possible observations. Every conceivable observation can be fitted into it. It is thus 'outside of empirical science' but not necessarily false. *No one can think of ways to test it.* Ideas, either without basis or based on a few laboratory experiments carried out in extremely simplified systems, have attained currency far beyond their validity. *They have become part of an evolutionary dogma* accepted by most of us as part of our training.[10] (My italics)

Fortunately for the image of science, the general public is largely unaware of what is going on. There is something unseemly about a situation where some scientists declare, with great emphasis, 'Evolution is a dead cert – a stone sober fact,' while others reply, 'Oh, no it isn't – it's just a clever theory that might or might not turn out to be true.'

Make no mistake, it is not only the prejudice and dogmatism of some Christians that makes a sober reappraisal of evolution difficult. There is plenty of unreasonableness and fizz on the part of scientists, too.

Facing the facts

So we are going to try and take a fresh look, an honest and impartial look, at the subject of evolution. This is not going to be easy. I shall probably bring down wrath upon my head from all sides: from fervent fundamentalists, mellow modernists and bigoted biologists alike. Not to worry – the job has got to be done. Let's get on with it.

The first thing to note is that evolution has been shown to work, up to a point. Why are there so many different kinds of roses in our gardens? Why are there dogs to suit all tastes, from the pocket-sized chihuahua to the fearsome wolfhound? Because over a long period men have caused them to evolve, by selecting as their breeding stock roses and dogs with those characteristics that they wanted to emphasise.

These are examples of evolution by deliberate human selection, and we now have a fair idea of how it works. Animals and vegetables are made up of microscopic building-bricks called cells, and inside every cell are some enormous molecules of a chemical called DNA.

By 'enormous' I mean enormous as molecules go, of course; they are far too small to be seen, even with a good optical microscope, but they are made up of many thousands of atoms stuck together. Thus they are thousands of times as big as molecules of simple chemicals such as oxygen (2 atoms), water (3 atoms) and ammonia (4 atoms).

These thousands of atoms in a DNA molecule can be strung together in an endless number of different ways, just as you can string thousands of words together to make an endless number of different books. But you cannot write books by throwing words together at random: you have to abide by the rules of grammar and common sense. Similarly, DNA is not composed of atoms joined together any old how. The rules of DNA grammar are quite strict, but even so there are *billions* of different kinds of DNA in the world today, and countless billions more are theoretically possible.

As a matter of fact, the DNA in your own body is a unique chemical. Everybody else has DNA very similar to your own, but nobody has DNA quite like yours (unless you happen to be an identical twin). Each of the billions of molecules of DNA in your body is a complete blueprint of yourself, or to be more precise, of yourself as you were at birth, before experience began to fashion you.

This has to be so, because originally you were just a single, solitary cell. The DNA in that cell had to contain a complete set of instructions, to tell that cell how to develop into a human being – and not just any human being, but YOU, complete with all those characteristics you have inherited from your mother, and all those others in which you take after your father or your Great-Aunt Agatha.

That first cell was formed by the merging of two cells, one from each of your parents' bodies. But that initial merging of cells was not a simple event like the blending together of two eggs when you start to make an omelette. It was a far more complicated process than the total integration of two giant industrial corporations.

During this merger the many molecules of DNA from your mother linked up with an equal number of molecules of your father's DNA, to form a chemical that the world had never seen before – your very own DNA.

Usually the DNA in the father's germ cell is a good representation of his normal DNA, and the mother's is a good representation of hers. The result is a normal fertilised egg-cell, which should develop into a normal child. But occasionally something goes amiss. Just as a copy-typist can get a word wrong here and there, so the body's mechanism for copying DNA is not perfect. (Fair play to the body, though: it copies DNA far more efficiently than anyone can type!)

The occasional copying error in a DNA molecule is what biologists call a mutation. When this occurs in a reproductive cell the offspring does not take after its parents in quite the way it should.

It is this that has made plant-breeding and animal-breeding possible. If, in the germ cell of a dog, the bit of DNA that should say, 'Legs two feet long', accidentally says, 'Legs one foot six inches long', the result is a litter of shorter-than-usual dogs. The breeder wanting a dog small enough to go down foxholes selects these unusual dogs to breed from. Eventually, many generations and several copying errors later, the first fox terrier is born.

From deliberate selection to natural selection

Darwin had never heard of DNA. He was a hundred years too early for that. But he knew that *something* was causing mutations, and that by selecting from these it was possible to breed new kinds of plants and animals. At this point his mind took one of those daring leaps into the unknown that are the mark of genius.[11]

Could something in nature be doing just what plant and animal breeders do, only much more slowly? Was there some natural force taking advantage of small mutations and selectively breeding new species from them?

Darwin concluded that there was. The struggle to survive in a hard world would provide just such a force, naturally selecting those products of mutation that had some advantage over their competitors.

He noted that the environment was continually changing. Places always seemed to be getting warmer, or cooler, or wetter, or drier, or dustier, or something. In a changing world, those mutations that were better suited to the new environment would survive. Thus, mutations plus new environments plus natural selection would eventually produce new kinds of living things.

There is no doubt whatsoever that this sort of thing really does happen. It has been observed many times.

In the nineteenth century hideous concentrations of industry sprang up in the north of England, and the smoke from a forest of factory chimneys soon coloured the area around Manchester a sooty black. One day in 1850 somebody in this drab district caught a most unusual specimen of a Peppered Moth.

This creature is called 'Peppered' because its wings are a speckly brown. In normal circumstances this is the ideal colour for a moth, since it looks very like the bark of trees. Consequently a Peppered can sit on a tree trunk almost under a bird's nose without being noticed – and as birds are very fond of moths, the Peppered has not the least desire to draw attention to himself.

Now this particular Peppered was not the usual shade. It was black. Evidently some moth's DNA had become slightly garbled at one point, and the instruction, 'Wings speckled brown', had become, 'Wings jet black'.

In a normal countryside these poor little negroes would have been about as well camouflaged as the Eiffel Tower, and the birds would soon have put paid to that particular variety. But in sooty Manchester it was the ordinary, brown Peppereds that were having a job to hide from the birds. The black ones were as happy as a fish in water, and by the beginning of this century they were well established in many industrial areas.

A similar effect has occurred in the world of germs. Man introduced penicillin, and new strains of bacteria promptly evolved that are resistant to it. Man countered with other types of antibiotic, and the microbes replied by evolving varieties that could resist these also. The same sort of evolution has led to new varieties of rat that can laugh at rat-poison, and insects which can tolerate insecticides.

If mutations and natural selection can account for that much evolution within a few years, think what they might do over many millions of years. Isn't it possible that they could, in the long run, have produced all the different forms of life on earth, as Darwin suggested?

Before you plunge in with your own answer to that question, be it 'Yes' or 'No', bear one thing in mind. Taking a limited piece of information and applying it to a much larger area of application is quite a widely used technique. Engineers call it 'scaling up'; scientists call it 'extrapolation'.

When students are being trained to use the method they are warned that sometimes it works, but sometimes it fails miserably. It all depends on circumstances.

For example, suppose a man says, 'I have proved I can walk ten miles in a day and swim ten miles in a day. Don't you think it possible that, given enough time, I could walk the 3,000 miles across America and swim the 3,000 miles across the Atlantic?'

The answer is obviously: America, yes; Atlantic, no. Both extrapolations involve a scaling factor of 300 to 1, but one works and one doesn't.

27

So before we decide whether our experience of small-scale evolution is a reason for believing in large-scale evolution, let us be careful. It might be right, or it might not. For the moment it is best to leave the question wide open, and go on to lock at some more facts.

Evolution and geology

I want, at this point, to address a few words about geology to my Christian friends. Evolution has a very obvious connection with geology, and especially with palaeontology, the branch of geology concerned with fossils. It is a pity that this leads many non-scientists to confuse the two, since there is, in fact, a tremendous difference in outlook between them. Let me try and illustrate it.

If the police discover a dead body with brutally inflicted wounds on it they have only one ultimate aim: to establish the truth. Often there are no witnesses to such a crime and no confession, and in such cases a conviction can only be based upon circumstantial evidence. This means that proof of a criminal's guilt has to depend upon deductions, which are made from the acknowledged facts of the case.

So the police begin by bringing in their forensic scientists to investigate the scene of the crime. In particular, a thorough examination of the body is made to ascertain how long it has been dead.

Now let's suppose that in a case of this kind suspicion is focused upon your friend John Doe. He has a perfect alibi for the period from three p.m. until long after the body was found, but he cannot establish his whereabouts before three.

Unfortunately for him the doctor who examined the body at five o'clock estimated that it had been dead for six hours. The murder occurred at about eleven, when John might have been anywhere. What is worse, John

28

Doe's fingerprints were found on the dead man's garden gate.

If you wanted to defend John Doe it would be a waste of time to question the evidence of the police scientists. One man's fingerprints can be mistaken for another's, but this is so very unlikely that the possibility is not worth considering. Methods of ascertaining a time of death have been shown by numerous experiments to be reasonably accurate. An estimate of six hours dead might mean that death actually took place five hours earlier, or seven. But it could not possibly have been two hours, the time that would fit in with John's alibi.

The best thing you can do for John Doe is to accept the findings of the police doctors and fingerprint experts. Those can be regarded as facts. The weak points in the police case are the *deductions* that they base on those facts. Although John has no alibi, that does not make him guilty, since innocent men often have no alibis. His fingerprints on the gate do not prove that he entered the house; he might have touched the gate absent-mindedly as he walked up the street.

The analogy is not perfect, but it is not very wide of the mark. Geology is a science rather similar to the detective work practised by police scientists. Rocks are *things*: solid objects that can be examined, tested, experimented on, passed from one worker to another. The conclusions of geologists can, to a very considerable extent, be checked for accuracy.

Geological dating

Perhaps the most questionable parts of geology are the dates, which are bound to be lacking in absolute proof. But even these are based upon many different methods of establishing the ages of rocks, and the results are generally in very rough agreement with each other. This suggests that geological dating is not likely to be too far removed from the truth.

A rock dated at 100 million years old could perhaps turn out to be 200 million or 50 million years old. It might just conceivably be only 10 million. But it would be absurd to declare that it is really only about 10 *thousand* years old. Assertions like that do the Christian cause far more harm than good.[12]

It is, of course, quite possible from a Christian point of view that God has been carrying out creative work on a large scale fairly recently. If so, His activities may well have upset some of the geologists' calculations. It is not a bad idea to bear that possibility in mind. But remember, it is nothing more than a possibility, or what scientists would call an 'unverified hypothesis'. That means it cannot reasonably be used in an argument to oppose an accepted view. Geological dates are best accepted as being probably about right, unless and until some new evidence arises to cast doubt upon them.

The theory of large-scale evolution is a very different matter. While geology deals with solid *things*, evolution is concerned with *events*. The emergence of a new species is a kind of historical event, and unlike a piece of rock it cannot be experimented upon. All you can do about it is to make deductions, based upon such facts as are accessible today.

So if you ever have to defend a John Doe, don't attack what the police pathologists and fingerprint men regard as the facts of the case. Concentrate upon the deductions that the lawyers try to base upon those facts.

And if you want to defend your belief in your Creator, don't try to overturn the conclusions of the geologists[13] – they are much too well supported by experiments. Instead, focus your attention on the deductions that evolutionists make from the geological evidence.

The record of the rocks

From the available evidence it looks as if the earth is a few thousand million years old. For a very long time it seems to have been completely lifeless. Nobody can say when life first appeared, because the first living creatures were exceedingly small. Many of the oldest known fossils are so tiny they can only be seen under a microscope, and naturally they take a lot of finding. They are thought to be at least a thousand million years old.

It was not until about 600 million years ago that life really took off. Many different forms of life appeared, including creatures as elaborate as shellfish. These were a tremendous advance on the primitive creatures that preceded them, and the relatively sudden appearance of all these living things at about this time is one of the greatest unsolved problems in all science.

It seems that from then on life gradually became more and more advanced. True fish appeared more than 400 million years ago, and soon afterwards came the first land animals and elaborate plants. Small reptiles appeared a little later, and then the giant dinosaurs which were lording it over the earth 200 million years ago.

Soon after that the first birds and mammals arrived. Among the latecomers were the great apes. Later still – perhaps around a million years ago – there were ape-like creatures bearing a superficial resemblance to men. As time went by this resemblance seems to have grown stronger and stronger, although the first creature that we should have felt at home with was New Stone Age Man, who apparently came upon the scene a mere 12,000 years ago.

When the story of the earth is put like that, it certainly seems as if large-scale evolution, or something very like it, has occurred.

That's the nub of the matter. Evolution, or *something very like it*. Which is it?

The dumb cop

He seems to turn up in nearly every detective story. Perhaps he comes from the local police station, or perhaps from Scotland Yard. Either way he represents the Establishment – and like most Establishment figures in fiction, he's a clown.

The dumb cop arrives early at the scene of the crime. Painstakingly he gathers clues for a while, until finally he confesses himself satisfied. He pompously explains where all the evidence points and says whom he proposes to arrest.

His argument is plausible, but the reader is not taken in by it, because everybody knows the first rule of crime fiction is that the dumb cop is always wrong. Soon the brilliant amateur sleuth will appear on the scene. You can rely upon him to find the vital clues that the professional overlooked and to produce a new explanation of the evidence, thus finding the real criminal.

All good clean fun – and most unlike real life, of course.

And yet it is not entirely unlifelike. If we can but recognise it, there is a caricature of ourselves – of all of us – in that poor dumb detective. Human beings do tend to make their minds up too quickly, taking into account only those facts that they know about, and forgetting that new facts may turn up tomorrow.

Scientists are aware of this pitfall and try to avoid falling into it. In principle, they say, 'The views I hold today are tentative, based upon the evidence now available. If any new evidence comes along I shall, if necessary, change my views.'

In practice it does not always happen like that. Men of science are only human, after all, and history contains many examples of prominent scientists who clung obstinately to their early views, long after those views had been shown to be wrong.

Sometimes those wrong views have been totally and absurdly wrong. One such was the theory that lowly forms of life, such as bacteria and maggots, were generated spontaneously in decaying food – a sort of daily occurrence of the creation of life. Astonishing as it now seems, quite a number of influential biologists still believed this in Darwin's day.

A recent example relates to a remarkable new substance called 'polywater'. The renowned Russian scientist, Derjaguin, reported its discovery in 1967. He explained how water in very fine glass tubes turned into a treacly sort of material, which was as different from water as ice is, but was still only water in another form, just as ice is.

This new form of water was named 'polywater' because it was believed to be what chemists call a polymer, that is to say, a substance in which lots of ordinary water molecules cling together like the links of a chain to form a much smaller number of super-molecules. Hundreds of scientists started experimenting with this remarkable new material. During the next six years scores of scientific papers were published describing the results of these experiments, and providing brilliant theoretical 'explanations' of its molecular structure.

Then in 1973 Derjaguin published another paper[14] admitting it was all a ghastly mistake. 'Polywater' was not a polymer at all. It was nothing more than ordinary water, heavily contaminated with impurities washed out of the glass tube in which it was contained.

In other words, this wonderful new substance on which so much scientific manpower had been expended turned out to be merely a transparent form of mud!

So near and yet so far

More often, the wrong views were only a little bit wrong. They just needed one small adjustment to make them right.

My favourite example of this is Dante's theory of the universe, which is illustrated in Figure 1. This medieval Italian poet was also something of a scientist, or perhaps what we today might call a philosopher with scientific leanings.

Although many people in AD 1300 believed the world to be flat, Dante and numerous others knew it to be a globe.[15] What was more remarkable was the way he placed the heavenly bodies in orbits around the earth. He was terribly wrong in making our planet the centre of his universe – and yet he was astonishingly right in almost everything else.

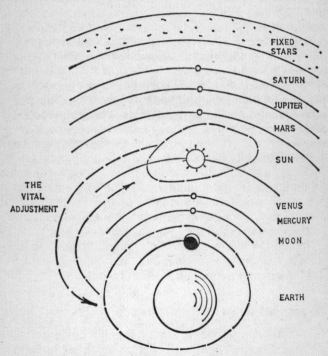

Figure 1. Dante's view of astronomy (AD 1300)
—hopelessly wrong, yet almost right.

Following the second-century Egyptian scientist, Ptolemy, Dante treated the moon as the nearest body to the earth (which it is), and the fixed stars as the most distant bodies (which they are). In between he had the orbits of the five visible planets, and he placed them in exactly the right order, with Mercury in the innermost orbit, Venus next, then Mars, then Jupiter, and finally Saturn. He even knew enough to place correctly the orbits of Mercury and Venus *between* us and the sun, and the orbits of the other planets *beyond* the sun.[16]

Hopelessly wrong – and yet astonishingly close to the truth. All that Dante's scheme needs to make it right is one adjustment. Take the earth, complete with its moon, and make it change places with the sun. That done, the universe of Ptolemy and Dante becomes the same as that of twentieth-century science.

Perhaps – and I am not prepared to say more than perhaps at this stage of the book – perhaps the theory of total evolution may be rather like that. Perhaps evolution also is astonishingly close to the truth, and yet dreadfully wrong.

Let us at least keep an open mind as to that possibility.

Chapter 3

EXPERT WITNESSES

Every law court has its retinue of expert witnesses. Hand-writing experts, agricultural experts, explosives experts, aircraft experts ... you name them. In an unending procession they troop in and out of the witness box. The general public is suitably awed, for these are the *men who know*.

One of Britain's top legal men, however, is less impressed. To put it bluntly, he sounds as if he is thoroughly fed up with experts. Mr D. C. Anderson, Queen's Counsel and Chief Reporter for Public Inquiries in Scotland, recently announced in the court where he was presiding:

> You don't need to be in awe of experts. In about one-third of the thirty or so public inquiries I have taken I have found the experts to be wrong and John Citizen to be right ... Although experts can be of great assistance in their field, it is a very stupid expert who insists that he alone is right. You find experts on both sides at inquiries, one saying black and the other white.[1]

We must be fair to the experts. Mr Anderson was referring to what are known as 'expert opinions'. In his court of inquiry an expert had declared that a proposed new oil refinery would not produce a nasty smell in the Ayrshire village next door. A local inhabitant had said, 'Ah hae ma doots', and Mr Anderson was not so sure either.

Mr Anderson, who after all had admitted that experts 'can be of great assistance', would probably have agreed that experts are usually right when it comes to questions of fact.[2] It is when experts make deductions and give their opinions that they need watching.

In this chapter we shall observe a number of expert evolutionists in the witness box. Bear Mr Anderson's advice in mind as you consider what these experts have to say.

Scholarly bluffmanship

The late Jacques Monod is a good example of an expert who managed to overawe poor John Citizen, not to mention his fellow-countryman le pauvre Jean Citoyen. His book, *Chance and Necessity*, was published in French in 1970 and in English in 1972,[3] and it rapidly became a bestseller.

Reviews in the popular press were quite enthusiastic. According to the back cover of the paperback edition, *The Economist* described it like this: 'A great book, sinewy, lucid and intelligible, alike to the non-scientist and the novice in philosophy.'

I don't know how many 'non-scientists and novices in philosophy' rushed out and bought the book on the strength of that review. Nor do I know what they thought when they found the book was largely composed of paragraphs like this:

As the teleonomic properties of living beings appear to challenge one of the basic postulates of the modern theory of knowledge, any philosophical, religious, or scientific view of the world must, *ipso facto*, offer an implicit if not an explicit solution to this problem. Every solution in its turn, whatever the motivation behind it, just as inevitably implies a hypothesis as to the causal and temporal precedence, in relation to each other, of the two properties characteristic of living beings: invariance and teleonomy.[4]

Perhaps that is what *The Economist* calls 'sinewy'; I

wouldn't know. But I should not myself have praised it as 'lucid and intelligible'.

Be that as it may, the book sold well and Monod suddenly found himself one of the very small band of scientists whose names are known to the world at large. Evidently the book fulfilled a need. People who ploughed through it got the satisfaction of feeling they were engaged in a very learned exercise, and at least they gathered that Monod was making three main points:

> Science is Wonderful.
> Evolution is Unchallengeable.
> God is Non-Existent.

Monod had few dissatisfied customers, as the majority of his readers could say an enthusiastic Amen to each line of that incantation. A group of dissenters did publish a reply,[5] but nobody took much notice of it. Another evolutionist complained petulantly, 'I wish I was as sure of anything as Monod is of everything,'[6] but he too was a voice in the wilderness. Most commentators seem to have thought Monod's views were marvellous.

After all, Monod was a great biochemist who had won a Nobel prize for his research in molecular biology. Who would dare to disagree with an expert as distinguished as that?

Strange coincidence

By a remarkable coincidence a booklet by another highly distinguished biochemist was published in 1970, the same year as the original (French) edition of *Chance and Necessity*. His name is Professor Sir Ernst Chain, and like Monod he won a Nobel prize for his biological research work, in which he discovered the curative properties of penicillin.

Like Monod's book, Chain's booklet began life as a memorial lecture at a university. Again like Monod, Chain wrote about science, ethics and the destiny of man.[7]

There the similarity ends. While Monod's book asserts that the theory of total evolution has achieved 'full significance, precision and certainty,'[8] Chain says this:

> It is, of course, nothing but a truism, and not a scientific theory, to say that living systems do not survive if they are not fit to survive ... There is no doubt that such variants do arise in nature and that their emergence can and does make some limited contribution towards the evolution of species. *The open question is the extent and significance of their contribution* (my italics). To postulate ... that the development and survival of the fittest is *entirely* a consequence of chance mutations ... seems to me a hypothesis based on no evidence and irreconcilable with the facts ... These classical evolutionary theories are a gross oversimplification of an immensely complex and intricate mass of facts, and it amazes me that they were swallowed so uncritically and readily, and for such a long time, by so many scientists without a murmur of protest. However, at the present time an increasing number of scientists are rapidly becoming aware of the fact that *not all is well with the evolutionary theories and that these are, in fact, due for a drastic revision.*[9] (My italics)

Purpose in nature

Another difference between the two men is their attitude to the question of 'purpose'. As you might expect from its title, *Chance and Necessity* asserts that there is no purpose in the universe. Monod admits that living things *appear* to be built according to a plan, but argues that this appearance is deceptive. He says:

> The cornerstone of the scientific method is the postulate that nature is objective. In other words, the

systematic denial that 'true' knowledge can be reached by interpreting phenomena in terms of final causes – that is to say, of 'purpose' . . . It is obviously impossible to imagine an experiment proving the *nonexistence* anywhere in nature of a purpose, of a pursued end. But the postulate of objectivity is consubstantial with science . . . It is impossible to escape it, even provisionally or in a limited area, without departing from the domain of science itself.[10]

Notice how Monod lays the law down here. 'There is no purpose in nature. We can't prove this, but you must accept it on trust,' he says, in effect. 'Science itself depends on that assumption. You must accept it, or else you are no scientist.'

Most of Monod's readers, not knowing any better, will no doubt feel obliged to take his word for it. Yet what he says is quite untrue. Science makes no such assumption.

Science, as such, is entirely neutral on the subject of 'purpose'. Science gets on with its job of seeing *how* things work. It is not concerned with *why* they work, or why we are here at all.

Even so, many scientists are convinced that the apparent purposiveness of nature is real enough. Chain is one of them. He says:

The principle of teleological purpose [i.e. well-planned, creative purpose[11]] . . . stares the biologist in the face wherever he looks . . . The probability for such an event [i.e. the origin of DNA molecules by sheer chance] to have occurred is just too small to be seriously considered, given even a time period as long as that of the existence of life on earth. *The assumption of directive forces in the origin and development of vital processes becomes a necessity* in any kind of interpretation.[12] (My italics)

There's obviously something twisted about this world

of ours. Monod's adherents run into millions, while Chain's readers are numbered only in thousands.

And millions of people still go around telling those twentieth-century fairy tales, 'All biologists accept evolution as proven fact,' and, 'Science has shown that there is no God.'

Strange, isn't it?

Another straight-talking biologist

Evolutionists make a habit of overstating their case. Take this recent declaration, for instance, by the editor of *Nature*: 'Nobody in his senses can deny that the doctrine of evolution is an exceedingly powerful means of relating such a variety of phenomena that it deserves to be called the truth.'[13]

Observe the way the editor wields the big stick. 'Nobody in his senses can deny' that evolution should 'be called the truth', he says, thus putting us firmly in our place. If we dare to have any doubts about evolution, we are automatically listed as fit for the funny farm.

This is a downright insult to a number of eminent biologists, such as Professor G. A. Kerkut of Southampton University. His professional standing is such that he was appointed general editor of an important series of more than fifty textbooks on zoology.[14]

His own book in that series is entitled *Implications of Evolution*.[15] In the Preface he puts his cards on the table by admitting that he believes in evolution – but with serious reservations:

I believe that the theory of Evolution as presented by orthodox evolutionists is in many ways a satisfying explanation of some of the evidence. At the same time I think that the attempt to explain all living forms in terms of evolution *from a unique source* ... is premature and not satisfactorily supported by present-day evidence. ... The supporting evidence remains to be

41

discovered ... I for one do not think that it has been proven beyond all reasonable doubt ... It is very depressing to find that many subjects are being encased in scientific dogmatism.

In chapter 1 he discusses the history of our university system. Universities were originally church institutions, and in his view, 'many of the Church's worst features are still left embedded in present-day studies'. Today's biology student is not required to have an 'intelligent understanding' of what he is taught; he is treated as a mere 'opinion-swallowing grub' (p. 3).

So much for the popular idea that scientists are trained at university to think for themselves!

In chapter 2 Kerkut states his main thesis like this:

The evidence at present does not by any means exclude the concept that present-day living things have many different origins. If we do not hold that the origin of life was unique ... there is the alternative point of view. *This is that living things have been created many times* (p. 13, my italics).

(The word 'created' does not necessarily mean, 'created *by God*', of course; Professor Kerkut, in fact, does not believe in God.)

In succeeding chapters Kerkut shows that there is, indeed, biological evidence to support the view of multiple creation. Time after time, when discussing various aspects of the usual evolutionary theory, he makes statements like this:

Nothing is definite; all is hypothesis and opinion (p. 25).

The information at our disposal is not sufficient to allow us to come to any definite conclusion (p. 35).

We can if we like, *believe* that one or other of the

various theories is the more correct, but we have no real evidence (p. 49).

Many of the conclusions that we have today are only tentative ones (p. 141).

It is a matter of faith that the textbook pictures are true, or even that they are the best representations of the truth that are available to us at the present time (p. 148).

It is a matter of belief which way the evidence happens to point. As Berrill states, 'in a sense this account is science fiction' (p. 153).

In the last four pages of Kerkut's book he summarises his general conclusions. The most interesting of these is as follows:

It seems at times as if many of our modern writers on evolution have had their views by some sort of revelation ... It is premature, not to say arrogant, on our part if we make any dogmatic assertion as to the mode of evolution of the major branches of the animal kingdom (p. 155, my italics).

And these are not the views of a Christian anxious to uphold his religious beliefs, but the views of an agnostic. Whatever bias Kerkut may have, it is certainly not a bias in favour of religion.

A generation ago

This sort of conflict is nothing new. There have always been two sorts of biologists.

On the one hand there have been those who have declared, probably in a loud voice and with a slightly red face, 'Evolution is proved. Everybody knows that. Stand up any dunce who disagrees!' Typical of that class was Professor Dobzhansky, who wrote nearly forty years ago:

43

No informed person entertains any doubt of the validity of the evolution theory in the sense that evolution has occurred. Evolution as an historical fact is established as thoroughly as science can establish a fact witnessed by no human eye.[16]

Typical of the other class was a contemporary of Dobzhansky, Dr W. R. Thompson, the former director of the Commonwealth Institute of Biological Control. When he died in 1972 his obituary in a scientific journal said:

Thompson's career ... was long and distinguished ... Many honours were accorded Thompson ... he won many awards and medals as tributes to his work ... With his death entomology has lost a personality whose impact in the field of biological control will be of lasting academic and economic value.[17]

In short, Thompson was a great biologist. It was for this reason that he was chosen by the publishers to write an introduction to a new edition of Darwin's book, *The Origin of Species*,[18] issued in 1956. People who had taken Professor Dobzhansky's word for it that 'no informed person entertains any doubt' must have had a shock when they picked up this edition of Darwin's famous book and read, in the very first paragraph of the Introduction: 'I am not satisfied that Darwin proved his point or that his influence in scientific and public thinking has been beneficial.'

Yes, you read it right. That is exactly what Thompson said. And he went on to explain why he said it, in one fascinating page after another. Here are just a few extracts:

Since he [Darwin] had at the time the *Origin* was published no body of experimental evidence to support his theory, *he fell back on speculative arguments* ... Personal convictions, simple possibilities, are presented as if they were proofs.

Darwin did not show in the *Origin* that species had originated by natural selection; he merely showed, on the basis of certain facts and assumptions, how this *might* have happened, and as he had convinced himself he was able to convince others.

Darwin in the *Origin* was not able to produce palae-ontological [i.e. fossil] evidence sufficient to prove his views ... *the evidence he did produce was adverse to them*; and I may note that *the position is not notably different today* ... The modern Darwinian palae-ontologists are obliged, just like their predecessors and like Darwin, to water down the facts. (My italics)

Why do they do it?

Now this is all very odd. As the old North Country fellow said, 'There's nowt so queer as folk.' But why do people react in such a curious way?

Since biologists of the stature of Sir Ernst Chain, Professor Kerkut and Dr Thompson have published such outspoken criticisms of evolutionary theory, why are their views swept under the carpet? Why do various other eminent biologists keep repeating the fairy tale, 'Evolution is a proven fact – every intelligent person knows that'?

And, above all, why do these others get away with it? Why are so many people gullible enough to believe them? Why?

There are quite a number of reasons. Habit, fashion and the desire to be in the swim must all play a part. But above all there are four special factors which load the scales in favour of evolution.

The first of these is one I can sympathise with up to a point: biology *needs* the theory of large-scale evolution to make it hang together. Without the theory, biology would just be an enormous collection of more or less unrelated facts.

Whereas, if a biologist believes that every living thing is directly related to every other living thing, then the situation is very different. For him, all biology is the study of one vast family, and he can sort out all his information by hanging it on the branches of one enormous family tree.

If you come to him and start asking awkward questions about evolution, you can hardly expect a warm welcome. The evolutionary family tree is the central framework of his science. If anyone should chop that tree down, much of his scientific knowledge would collapse in an untidy heap. The temptation for him to defend his evolutionary tree at all costs must be overwhelming.

The real world is very, very complicated. Because of this, and because we all like nice, tidy explanations, we usually tend to oversimplify things when we explain them. It follows that the more all-embracing a scientific theory can be made, the more popular it will prove – and the more likely it is to be wrong.

One of the greatest of philosophers, Bacon, warned us of this danger three-and-a-half centuries ago.[19] But mankind is slow to learn the lesson. The marvellous simplicity and comprehensiveness of the large-scale evolutionary theory make it terribly attractive, and so its devotees cheerfully ignore the possibility that it could well be a misleading oversimplification.

'Science is not like that'

There is a popular idea that 'science is only concerned with the truth'. True, or false?

Professor Roxburgh of London University spotlighted this question in a scientific journal a few years ago. This was his own answer: 'Science is not like that at all. There is a powerful establishment and a belief system. There are

46

power seekers and career men, and if someone challenges the establishment he should not expect a sympathetic hearing.'[20] In other words, science is not something outside the rat race, it is an integral part of it.

This is the second important factor to be reckoned with. Science has become an industry full of closed shops, each as cosy as a private yacht on a Mediterranean cruise. Woe betide anyone who dares to rock the boat!

Sir Peter Medawar said something similar in one of his Reith Lectures: 'Scientists tend not to ask themselves questions until they can see the rudiments of an answer in their minds. *Embarrassing questions tend to remain unasked*, or if asked, to be answered rudely'[21] (my italics).

Following in Old Bill's footsteps

Another facet of the same problem is the Old Bill syndrome. You may perhaps remember Bairnsfather's elderly private in World War I, sternly rebuking the young whippersnapper who dared to criticise the muddy shell-hole where they were sheltering from the enemy's fire: 'If you knows of a better 'ole, go to it.'

Biologists often take a very similar line: 'Don't just criticise evolution – give us a better scientific theory to put in its place.'

This is a ridiculous attitude. A rotten egg is a rotten egg, and the fact that you cannot lay a good egg is no reason to make you swallow a bad one. Yet enthusiastic Darwinists frequently resort to such arguments.

Professor D. M. S. Watson, for example, once said that evolution: '. . . is accepted by zoologists not because it has been observed to occur or . . . can be proved by logically coherent evidence to be true, but because the only alternative, special creation, is clearly incredible.'

Similarly, Sir Julian Huxley declared that: 'we must (*unless we confess total ignorance* and abandon for the time any attempts at explanation) invoke natural selection'[22] (my italics).

Poor old Socrates. It is two thousand four hundred years since he taught the world that the height of wisdom is to admit, 'I don't know.'

Yet still Sir Julian and the other Old Bills of modern science prefer to call a dubious theory a fact, rather than take Socrates' advice.

A new religion

The fourth vital factor is the way in which large-scale evolution has become a kind of substitute religion for many biologists. At least one leading evolutionist has admitted this in as many words: 'The concept of organic evolution is very highly prized by biologists, *for many of whom it is an object of genuinely religious devotion*, because they regard it as a supreme integrative principle'[23] (my italics).

Dr Thompson was very well aware of this tendency. In his introduction to Darwin's *Origin*, from which I have already quoted, he also remarked: 'The doctrine of evolution by natural selection as Darwin formulated, and as his followers still explain it, has a strong anti-religious flavour ... For the majority of its readers the *Origin* effectively dissipated the evidence of providential control.'

In other words, Darwinism makes an ideal foundation for atheism, as we saw in chapter 2. It is not a coincidence that the most fervent evolutionists – for instance, Huxley, Waddington and Wells, – are often what you might call dedicated atheists.

The fashionable way of life for atheists today is called 'Humanism', which is a kind of religion without God. Sir Julian Huxley's book on humanism is actually entitled, *Religion without Revelation*.

Another lengthy book setting out the Humanist creed[24] employs the word 'evolution' six times on the very first page. The blurb on the dust jacket tells us in its opening paragraph: 'Evolutionary humanism ... is

48

emerging as the new system of thought and belief concerned with our destiny. Man is a natural phenomenon produced by the evolutionary process . . .'

It is not surprising that a great many biologists are unbelievers. The appeal of a career in biology is a magnet for young atheists, since evolutionary theory provides them with a delightful justification for their beliefs.

Even among those biologists who believe in God, you often see signs of this semi-religious devotion towards evolution. For example, Professor Sir Alister Hardy, a biologist who holds a very liberal form of Christian belief, says of another believer, Teilhard de Chardin, that he '. . . believes passionately that God must be linked with biological evolution. This indeed is an intuitive step in the right direction.'[25] Note that revealing word, 'passionately'. This is not the language of a cool-thinking scientist; it suggests rather a man who has been swept off his feet by a popular form of near-idolatry.

People are usually touchy about their religion, and in circles where evolution is a pseudo-religion its defenders are as prickly as porcupines. A few years ago a foremost British evolutionist admitted that: 'Neo-Darwinism has become an established orthodoxy, any criticism of which is regarded as little less than *lèse majesté* [i.e. treason].[26]

Incidents are constantly occurring that prove the truth of these words. Here is just one recent example.

In 1974 a Japanese biologist, Tomoko Ohta, published a review paper in a British journal. She began the paper like this: 'As more data accumulate on evolutionary change at the molecular level, it becomes increasingly necessary to re-examine evolutionary theories . . .'[27]

This did not go down at all well. The last thing most British evolutionists want to do is to 're-examine evolutionary theories'. This Japanese lady was threatening to upset their applecart, and they were duly disturbed.

One of them published a reply in a later issue of the

49

same journal. In this he described Ohta's views as 'potentially dangerous to our science'.[28]

Science writer Nigel Calder seized on this revealing phrase and wrote a letter to the Editor condemning such a pathetic attitude. In it he said: 'If science does not live dangerously, always open to rebuttal and revision, it quickly ceases to be science. Neo-Darwinism has already shown signs of hardening into *quasi-religious dogma* ... some of the critics of Kimura and Ohta react like *priests scenting blasphemy*'[29] (my italics).

This is not an isolated instance. It is obvious to anyone who reads biological literature with an open mind that evolution is different from all the other branches of science.

I would not go so far as to use the term that some critics of evolution use: science-fiction. But evolution certainly deserves the description of 'science-faith'.

What has all this proved?

At this point it may be useful to take stock and try to see what we have learned.

First and foremost, we have seen that biology today is in a state of almost unbelievable confusion where evolution is concerned. Some prominent evolutionists keep thumping the rostrum and preaching to their disciples that evolution is an established fact. Meanwhile, other distinguished biologists are quietly proclaiming that evolution is only an unproved theory – and a very questionable one at that.

Beware of jumping to the conclusion that evolution has been proved false. It hasn't. To say that it has is to act as unreasonably as those bigoted evolutionists who say it has been proved true.

The fact is that the theory of large-scale evolution is still on trial. There is a lot to be said for it – and a great deal that can be said against it, too. That is why some biologists believe in it and others do not.

In the circumstances it is obviously unwise to be dogmatic about it. We simply do not have nearly enough information to reach a final conclusion.

The wisest course is to put evolution quietly on the shelf, and label it, 'An interesting, but speculative and totally unproved theory; to be re-examined when more facts emerge.'

Personally I imagine that the theory will turn out to be not just unproved, but unprovable. But that remains to be seen. For the present the one really important fact is this: evolution is still an unproved theory.

Like some television programmes, the theory of large-scale evolution is extremely popular because it *looks* good and gives pleasure, and not because it *is* good through and through.

Giant confidence trick

This simple fact, that evolution is just an unproved hypothesis (which is a scientific way of saying, 'an intelligent guess'), is of tremendous importance. It means that the case for God's existence based on nature remains unanswered.

It is still a perfectly valid argument to say, 'Look at this superbly wonderful world around you. If God did not make it, what did?'

It is no use for the unbeliever to reply triumphantly, 'Evolution produced it!' as if that settled the matter. Evolution is only a hypothesis, and a hypothesis settles nothing.

Admittedly, the unbeliever may retort that the existence of God is also only a hypothesis. From his point of view this is so.

What this means is that we now have two hypotheses, which for the moment must be treated with equal respect. One hypothesis says that everything in the universe just evolved on its own. The other hypothesis says that everything somehow owes its existence to the creative activity of God.

Now we can begin to look at this marvellous world in more detail, to see which of those two alternatives is more likely.

Chapter 4

THE JUST-SO WORLD

When I was a boy we knew a useful trick for watching wildlife. Four boys would go together into a thicket where birds were nesting. The birds would all fly off with a great commotion, and then one boy used to hide under a bush while the other three marched away. As soon as they were a safe distance off the birds would return, blissfully unaware of the boy in the bush.

Our theory was that birds cannot count up to four. They would say to themselves (or so we imagined), 'Boys went in – boys went out – therefore no boys still there.'

Whether this was the way it worked or not, the fact remains that birds and animals have a very limited ability to grasp the significance of numbers. But then so do we humans where very large numbers are concerned.

This is a pity, because it means that we are quite unable to comprehend the awesome size of the universe. Confronted with the figures, the human mind can't even be bothered to boggle: it just gives up.

Suppose we start trying to draw a map of the universe. If we put two dots on it an inch apart, they will represent the earth and the sun on a scale of about one inch to ninety-two million miles. Some map.

Now, where do we put dots to represent the stars? Unfortunately they are all a long way off the edge of the paper. If we only wanted to include the very nearest star of all, we should still need a map that was four miles long.

The centre of the group of stars, or galaxy, where we live, would be about 25,000 miles off the map. And our galaxy is only one tiny corner of the universe. Thousands of millions of galaxies have been discovered, each containing thousands of millions of stars. That means countless millions of millions of millions of stars in the *known* universe. And how much more universe there is out of sight is still a matter of controversy.

You see what I meant by the mind being unable to grasp numbers like this? All we can safely say is that the universe is unimaginably large.

Our expanding universe

It is not easy to believe that there is a God who is great enough and wise enough and powerful enough to create this gigantic universe.

Yet what are the alternatives? Either that nothing created it – that it just sprang into existence on its own, so to speak – or that it has always existed. Neither of those possibilities is any easier to believe in than God; the plain fact is that the riddle of the universe's existence has no easy solution, whether we believe in God or not.

Science can only offer us a very limited amount of help with the problem. The study of the universe and its origin is called cosmology, and there are many things that this branch of science cannot do.

In particular, cosmology cannot tell us how or why the universe first began, or what there was in its place before that. Nor do we know whether the universe stretches out for ever, or whether it has boundaries, or what lies beyond those boundaries if they exist.

The main thing cosmology can do is to explain what is going on in the universe at the present time. And what we now know is fascinating.

First of all, the galaxies are moving away from each other at enormous speeds; in other words, the universe is expanding.

This discovery has provided cosmologists with their biggest problem. Obviously, the universe cannot have been expanding for ever; it looks as if the galaxies were once very close together and started moving outwards. If this is so, what was it that set them going?

Scientists are often reluctant to answer a question like

that by saying, 'The Creator'. But this is not because there is any scientific reason to think that it wasn't the Creator. It is simply because, as soon as a scientist says, 'The Creator did it', he is liable to stop asking questions as to how it happened – and scientists naturally want to go on asking more questions and finding more answers. So they deliberately pass over the question of what (or who) started the universe going, and concentrate on studying how the start-up (or 'big bang') might have proceeded.

In addition, an enormous amount of mathematical effort has been expended trying to find other explanations of our expanding universe.

One alternative theory is that the expansion really has been going on for ever, in what is called a steady-state situation. According to this explanation, the universe is rather like a fountain in a pool, where water that overflows the edges of the pool reappears in the jets at the centre. Only in the universe it is whole galaxies that are supposed to be disappearing 'over the edge', while fresh matter keeps appearing 'in the middle'.

Another theory is that the universe is a bouncy one. According to this suggestion, it spends a while (not long – just a few thousand million years or so!) expanding; then it comes to rest and starts to contract again, until it is all very tightly packed; then it starts expanding again, and so on, for ever and ever.

At the time of writing it appears that neither of these alternative theories provides a satisfactory explanation.[1] And even if, one day, some mathematical genius produces a perfect explanation, it would still be only an explanation of what *might* have happened – there would be no way of proving that it really did happen. At present it looks very much as if the universe had a clearcut beginning – in other words, either a creation or something very much like it – about ten thousand million years ago.

Running down

Another important discovery is that the universe is running down. This has been known at least since the time of Newton. He observed that unless energy is continuously supplied hot bodies always cool down whilst cold ones grow warmer, and he concluded, reasonably enough, that the universe must once have been created with a store of usable energy which is now being used up.[2]

Two centuries later this simple fact was expressed in mathematical terms, in what is now known as the Second Law of Thermodynamics. Wherever we look in the universe we see examples of this principle.

Our sun, for instance, like most other stars, is composed mainly of hydrogen, which is steadily being converted into helium. It is this 'burning' of hydrogen that produces the sun's heat and light; when all the usable hydrogen is spent the sun will explode or die. (Don't panic: there is enough hydrogen left to last for millions of years.)

So the universe is rather like a ship in mid-ocean, with its fuel tanks half full and its stores half consumed. In the case of the ship we know that somebody must have fuelled and provisioned it at the start of the voyage. But who originally filled up the 'fuel tanks' of the universe with hydrogen fuel, and provided all the necessary conditions for that fuel to be turned into heat at an appropriate rate?

There are still a great many scientists who answer that question the same way as Newton did: the Creator.

But there are many others who would answer something like this: 'We don't know. Perhaps we never shall know. But it simply *can't* be the Creator – you see, I don't believe in Him!'

It is not very difficult to decide which of those two answers makes more sense.

Those microscopic building bricks

If the size of the universe takes your breath away, the smallness of atoms is absolutely staggering.

A speck of dust too small to be seen without a microscope could have a million million atoms in it. A single drop of water contains more than 1,000,000,000,000,000,000,000 atoms.

Originally, men thought these tiny building bricks of matter were as solid as billiard balls, but now we know differently. Atoms are in fact composed almost entirely of empty space.

This is because they are made up of a number of other particles, very much smaller than themselves. Electrons, for example, are so small that if you were to pack them cheek by jowl (which you can't, of course) you would need 1,000,000,000,000,000 of them to occupy as much space as one typical atom.

But the most interesting thing about these fundamental particles is not their minute size. It is the way in which their arrangement within the atom gives rise to all the various properties of the hundred-or-so basic chemical substances that we call elements.

Why is oxygen a gas? Because of the way the sub-atomic particles are arranged in the oxygen atom. Why is iron a strong metal? Because of the arrangement of the particles in its atom. Why is water wet? Because of the make-up of the oxygen and hydrogen atoms of which it is composed. And so on, right through all the substances in the universe.

Of all such questions, perhaps the most interesting is this: why does the element carbon, unlike any other element, possess the property of joining on to itself to an almost unlimited extent, so that enormously long chains of carbon atoms can easily be formed?

Two very different answers are possible. Either (1) Because of the way the electrons behave in the carbon atom; or (2) Because it appears that life would be impossible if carbon did not have that property. Scientists cannot conceive how any advanced form of life at all could exist without long-chain carbon compounds.

Answer (1) is safe, sound and not a bit controversial. But it does not really tell us very much. It amounts to a statement that that's the way things are; they just happen to be like that.

Answer (2) is quite thrilling. It informs us that our very existence depends upon the extraordinary behaviour of the carbon atom. At the same time it stirs up a hornet's nest of controversy. It implies that carbon's unique properties were built into it for a purpose. It is, in fact, the sort of answer that only a believer in God would give.

But is it an unreasonable answer? If you disallow it, there is only one alternative: carbon's remarkable properties exist by sheer chance.

All right, perhaps they do. As the card player said when his partner dealt him the ace of trumps for the third time running, 'I can believe in flukes as long as they don't happen too often.'

Let's see if there are any more flukes like that.

Luck, or design?

Another element with a unique property is phosphorus. Its electrons are arranged in such a way that large quantities of energy are stored when a phosphorus atom hangs on to another atom, under certain conditions.

All animal muscles operate by using this kind of energy, stored temporarily in a chemical called adenosine triphosphate, or ATP for short. Without phosphorus and its exceptional energy-storing ability it is unlikely that any kind of higher animal could possibly live.

Of all the chemical elements there is only one with this extraordinary property. Yet there simply had to be one such element, or we should not be here.

How does it come about that this vitally important

element exists? Was it designed for the purpose it served? Or is this just another fluke?

Another remarkable substance is water, which, as everybody knows, is called H_2O because it is composed of two atoms of hydrogen (H) and one of oxygen (O).

Life revolves around water. Nothing can live without it because all living things are largely composed of water. Is this merely something peculiar to our own planet? Is it possible that in another world life of another kind exists, where water is a deadly poison and everybody drinks, shall we say, paraffin oil, because in that world plants and animals are based on paraffin instead of water?

No, this is science fiction of the wildest kind; in the real universe it is quite impossible. It is no coincidence that life in our planet is centred on water. When any acid reacts with any alkaline substance, water is formed. And vast numbers of vital chemical reactions will not take place at all unless water is present to help them along.

So it is not only life as we know it that revolves around water. The whole of chemistry also is centred on water. Matter being what it is, life – any sort of life based on matter – would simply have to employ water as its base. There is no choice.

This being so, it is extremely fortunate for us that water happens to possess a number of quite unexpected, extraordinary properties.

The strange ways of water

To begin with, the water molecule (H_2O) is a very small molecule indeed. It actually weighs much less than a molecule of oxygen (O_2) or a molecule of nitrogen (N_2), the two main gases in the air. And very small molecules invariably form gases, not liquids. Why, then, is water not a gas?

Water is a liquid because its molecules possess the strange ability to bunch together in small groups. Consequently, liquid water behaves as if it were really, say,

$2 \times (H_2O)$ or $3 \times (H_2O)$, that is to say, like H_4O_2 or H_6O_3, instead of simple H_2O. If this were not so, water would be a liquid only at temperatures far colder than the North Pole – and at such temperatures chemical reactions grind to a halt, so life of any kind would be impossible.

But if water remained as H_4O_2 and H_6O_3 when it evaporates, then water vapour would be much heavier than air. Consequently, it would hang around as a thick blanket of fog over the surface of the sea, high clouds could never form, weather as we know it would not exist, and life would certainly be very difficult if not impossible.

This does not happen, fortunately for us, because as soon as water evaporates the pairs and triplets of molecules split up. The H_4O_2 and H_6O_3 become simple H_2O again, and this is somewhat lighter than air – just enough to promote reasonable weather conditions on earth.

No other substance possesses this extraordinary property of being liquid at temperatures suitable for life, and at the same time forming a vapour that is lighter than air. That water should possess it is so surprising, so unforeseeable, that when it is pointed out to chemistry students for the first time they marvel at it. What a lucky thing for us that it does!

Another unique property of water is its ability to dissolve a vast range of solid chemicals. All the solid raw materials needed to build up a plant, or the body of an animal, have to be transported in solution, in the blood or the sap.

Thousands of vital chemicals are dissolved in your own bloodstream at this moment. No other liquid could dissolve half of them – except for savage substances like acids that would dissolve you as well. Water's solvent properties are one more remarkable fluke for which we can be very thankful.

Water is unique among common substances in at least

two other very important respects. It has an abnormally high specific heat capacity, which means that it holds heat better than almost anything else does. (Try filling your hot water bottle with oil, and see how quickly it cools down.) This helps to keep our country from going arctic every winter. Perhaps more important, it helps every animal to maintain a uniform temperature through the heat of the day and the chill of the night.

Finally, very cold water has the strange property of expanding as it gets colder, whereas practically everything else contracts as it cools. We are used to the fact that ice floats on water, but this is really a most exceptional phenomenon. By all the usual rules, ice ought to sink. (Try melting some fat in a chip pan, and see how the solid fat always goes to the bottom.)

Once more, it is very lucky for us that water is such a peculiar liquid. The expansion of water when it freezes breaks up rocks, and this is a vital factor in the production of fertile soil.

Fluke upon fluke upon fluke. One can't help wondering.

Is all this really coincidence? Or does Somebody keep dealing us good hands off the bottom of the pack?

Lucky planet earth

Lowly forms of life are not very choosy about the conditions in which they live. Some bacteria can survive being put in a deep freeze, while others somehow manage to make an honest living in steaming hot crude oil.

The highest forms of life, however, are much less tolerant. They like to have things just so: not too hot, not too cold, not too wet, not too dry, and so forth.

We can, of course, only speak precisely about life as we know it. But it is a fallacy to think that other forms of intelligent life might exist somewhere in the universe under extreme conditions. This almost certainly cannot be, because life – any kind of life employing any of the substances found in the universe – must be governed by the laws of physics and chemistry. And everything we know about the universe indicates that those laws hold everywhere.

Advanced life can exist on our planet because conditions are just right for it. We do not know how many planets there are in the universe, nor how many of them happen to have conditions suitable for supporting life. But we do know this: *the odds against the right conditions existing anywhere at all are enormous.* Let us consider just a few of the ways in which conditions on Planet Earth happen to be just right.

(1) *The right sort of sun*

Suns come in all sorts and sizes, from red giants to white dwarfs. Our sun is in nearly every respect a nice, happy medium: middle-aged, middle-sized, with a nice middle-of-the-range band of radiation. All this is just what the doctor ordered.

Many stars emit far too much death-dealing ultraviolet radiation, or an equally deadly form of nuclear radiation. Many emit far too little useful light to sustain plant life, and many others flare up at intervals, so that any planets they might have must be alternately scorched and frozen. A great many other stars have a twin star associated with them, whose heat would make life impossible on any planets in that solar system.

Our sun shines on us benevolently for century after century, with a benign, steady beam of just the right sort of radiation. Lucky us.[3]

(2) *The right distance from the sun*

There are nine planets in our solar system, spread out at widely differing distances from the sun. The furthest, Pluto, is a hundred times as far from the sun as the nearest, Mercury.

The two nearest planets to us are Venus, which is about three-quarters as far from the sun as we are, and Mars, which is about one-and-a-half times as far from the sun as ourselves. Spaceships full of scientific instruments have landed on those two neighbours of ours, so we know something about conditions there.

Venus is frightfully hot: temperatures up to about 500° C have been recorded on its surface.[4] Since boiling water is only 100° C, spacemen are not in a hurry to make a trip to Venus.

Mars is frightfully cold. The first spaceship to land there in 1976 recorded a temperature of −86° C at dawn; this is far colder than any temperature ever recorded in the Arctic.

Clearly, distance from the sun is very critical. Just a bit nearer to the sun, and Planet Earth's seas would soon be boiling; just a little farther out, and the whole world would become a frozen wilderness. What a good job our average distance from the sun is exactly right!

But that would not help us much if our orbit happened to be the wrong shape. All planets and satellites have orbits that are elliptical (oval) to some extent, and if our orbit were highly elliptical we should be at different distances from the sun at different times of the year. Then we should alternately freeze like Mars and fry like Venus once a year. Fortunately for us, our planet's orbit is very nearly a circle.

(3) *The right size*
The moon, which is just over a quarter the size of the earth, is a barren rock, for every scrap of air and water that it might once have possessed has been lost. Why? Because a body the size of the moon does not have enough gravity to hold liquids and gases on its surface. Even Mars, which is more than half the size of Earth, has only a trace of an atmosphere left.

On the other hand, it does not do for a planet to be too big. Large planets have a high force of gravity, so that objects on their surface weigh much more than they would on earth. This would make it very difficult for large animals (including ourselves) to get about. Even more serious, a big planet would probably retain in its atmosphere a number of poisonous lightweight gases, such as hydrogen, methane and ammonia, of which our own atmosphere is mercifully free.

Clearly, there is an ideal size for an inhabited planet. It needs to be just big enough to retain a respectable atmosphere, but no bigger. And Earth appears to be exactly the right size.

(4) *The right sort of rotation*

All the planets in the solar system rotate on their axes, but most of them rotate much more slowly than our own. Mercury takes 59 of our days to turn round once, while Venus takes 243 days.

Such slow rotation is extremely hostile to life. On earth it is usually much cooler at midnight than at midday, even though they are only twelve hours apart. But imagine a world where the day and the night each lasted for hundreds of hours: the days would be impossibly hot and the nights unbearably cold. (This is one of the factors leading to that frightening 500° C temperature measured on Venus.)

Nevertheless, it would not do for a planet to rotate very much faster than ours does, because this would probably cause appallingly fierce cyclones which would devastate the planet.

Evidently Planet Earth is in luck's way once more – its speed of rotation is not too fast, not too slow, but just right.

But speed is not everything. The direction of the axis of rotation is also very important, since this is what governs the intensity of summer and winter.

If a planet's axis of rotation is not tilted at all, there will be no summer and winter: the climate will be the same all the year round. Admittedly this would not make life impossible, although it would certainly be less interesting. But if the axis is tilted too much, as it is in the planet Uranus, then the winters would become killingly cold and the summers intolerably hot.

Planet Earth is fortunate in this respect, too. Its axis is tilted a comfortable 23.5° – just enough to produce well defined seasons with all their beneficial effects, but not enough to make either the Siberian winters or the Mediterranean summers unbearable.

(5) *Plenty of the right materials*

What are living things made of? First and foremost, they contain water – lots and lots of it. Apart from that, they are largely composed of the elements carbon, oxygen, nitrogen and hydrogen.

Of all those substances, only hydrogen is really abundant in the universe as a whole. So far as we can tell, the universe is very short of water, carbon, oxygen and nitrogen. Yet Earth – lucky, lucky Earth – has an abundance of all four of those life-giving substances.

Several other elements are needed in small quantities to sustain life. Phosphorus, potassium, iodine, chlorine, iron, calcium, sulphur, and a few others – we don't need much of them, but every form of life needs traces of some of them, and man needs a little of them all. How fortunate, then, that they are distributed widely enough for practically every living creature to have access to them.

(6) *Freedom from the wrong materials*

If you want living things to prosper it is not enough merely to supply the materials they need. You must also keep poisons well away from them. Heavy metals, such as arsenic, mercury and lead, can kill any advanced form of animal life. And again I don't mean 'life as we know it'; I mean 'life'. These metals are killers because they halt the essential chemical processes on which animal life depends. To say that Martians might thrive on arsenic is like saying that Martian motor cars might run very well on square wheels. Because of the laws of chemistry, any sort of advanced animal would be poisoned by these heavy metals.

Then there are the radioactive elements like uranium

and radium, They cause lots of mutations, most of them harmful. If they were plentiful, every child would be a thalidomide child – or worse. Advanced forms of life would soon die out under those conditions.

Fortunately for us, the heavy metals and the radio-active elements are not very plentiful on our planet. And most of what there is happens to be safely locked away in mineral deposits. It can't do any harm there (unless and until man digs it up and scatters it about).

Another remarkable feature of Planet Earth for which its inhabitants can be very thankful.

(7) *The right kind of sea*
Don't fall into the common mistake of underestimating the sea. It is one of the great wonders of the universe.

Some of its benefits are obvious. It provides a reservoir of water that is constantly evaporating and falling on the land as rain. And it acts also as a reservoir for heat, storing it up in the summer and releasing it in the winter.

Luckily for us, the sea is just about the right size to do both those jobs efficiently. It covers about four-fifths of the planet's surface, and if it occupied much less there would probably be a great deal more desert on the earth.

That is only the beginning of the story, though. One little-known function of the sea is keeping the composition of the air right. It is estimated that only 10 per cent of our oxygen is produced by the plants and trees on land; the other 90 per cent is said to come from the one-celled plants and seaweeds of the ocean.[5]

Another function of the sea is to receive the dirt and salts washed into it by rivers, much of which could be harmful if they remained on the land. But have you ever wondered why all this waste matter has not poisoned the sea? It has done just that to the Dead Sea; why not the great oceans also?

True, the oceans are a great deal larger than the Dead Sea. But they also receive the flow from a great many more rivers, and they have been in existence for very,

very much longer than the Dead Sea. Yet the oceans are nothing like as salty. Why?

This question has recently been the subject of much research, and an intriguing answer has emerged. There appear to be a number of automatic control systems operating in the ocean, which together keep the concentration of dissolved chemicals constant.[6] (A 'control system' is something like a thermostat, which keeps a room at a constant temperature by shutting off the heat automatically when the room gets a bit too hot, and turning it on again when it gets a little cooler.)

One such control system holds the phosphorus content of the sea at a steady level. It works like this. Microscopic plants feed on the dissolved phosphorus and turn it into an insoluble powder, which falls to the sea bed when the plant dies. If the phosphorus content rises, the plants multiply and remove the excess before it can poison the fishes; if it falls, some of the plants die and give the phosphorus a chance to build up again to its normal level.

Many other control mechanisms operate, so as to stabilise the entire chemical composition of the sea. To do their job they make use of plant life, fish life, and various chemical and geological effects.

The Dead Sea is a grim reminder of what happens to a body of water and its immediate surroundings when these control mechanisms break down. In the long run, not only all life in the sea depends on these remarkable control systems, but the very survival of life on our planet.

So it's very comforting to know that they work so well. Add them to the long list of things on earth that, by astonishing good fortune, happen to be just right.

(8) *The right kind of atmosphere*
Then there is the air we breathe. It contains roughly 78 per cent of nitrogen, 21 per cent of oxygen, 0.03 per cent of carbon dioxide, variable (small) amounts of water

vapour, and traces of several other gases that do not matter very much. But the ones mentioned are absolutely vital.

Take first that trifling 0.03 per cent of carbon dioxide. This is a waste product breathed out by animals; it is also an essential food for plants. Its concentration of 0.03 per cent is a perfect compromise between the needs of animal life and of plant life. Much more than this would be harmful to animals; but if there were any less, plants would be half starved.

The 21 per cent of oxygen is another critical figure. Animals would have difficulty breathing if the oxygen content fell very far below that value. But an oxygen level much higher than this would also be disastrous, since the extra oxygen would act as a fire-raising material. Forests and grasslands would flare up every time lightning struck during a dry spell, and life on earth would become extremely hazardous.

Fortunately, the oxygen content and the carbon dioxide content are both just right – and nature has its own control systems to make them stay that way.

Quantity of air is as important as quality. A planet can so easily have too much or too little of it. The atmosphere of Venus is a hundred times as thick as ours, and the life-giving rays of the sun cannot penetrate it. On Mars the air is a hundred times more rarefied than on Earth, and so is far too thin to sustain any elaborate forms of life.

But on our planet the density of the atmosphere, like almost everything else, is just right. There's no denying that Earth is an incredibly fortunate planet.

Missing the obvious

Scientists cannot help being impressed by the extraordinary collection of lucky coincidences affecting life on earth. It is a long list; there has not been space to put more than a small part of it in this chapter. Many scientists admit that it simply cannot be just a matter of luck, because the odds against that are so enormous.

It is interesting to see how non-believing scientists try to explain the situation once they have realised that so many flukes in a row demand an explanation. Here are three recent attempts.

F. J. Dyson writing in *Scientific American*, in a paper where he gave no indication of being a religious man, put it like this: 'As we look out into the universe and identify the many accidents of physics and astronomy that have worked together to our benefit, it almost seems as if *the universe must in some sense have known we were coming*'[7] (my italics).

The British cybernetician, Dr David Foster, has gone one better with a whole book on the subject, which he had entitled *The Intelligent Universe*.[8]

There is something rather pathetic about this approach. Scientists like Dyson and Foster seem unable to face the obvious conclusion that it looks as if some Supreme Being must be responsible for the design and maintenance of the universe. They evidently think that's too old fashioned.

So they propose a startling alternative: that the universe itself must be some sort of Supreme Being, responsible for its own design and maintenance. They seem to forget that there is nothing new about this notion, either. The ancient Greeks had a name for universe-worship which is still in use today – pantheism.

Dr James Lovelock and Dr Sidney Epton caused quite a stir in scientific circles in 1975 with a more original suggestion. In their paper, 'The Quest for Gaia',[9] they began by considering the conventional scientific attitude, which they summarised like this:

Life exists only because material conditions on Earth happen to be just right for its existence ... [this view] implies that *life has stood poised like a needle on its point for over 3,500 million years.* If the temperature or humidity or salinity or acidity or any one of a number of other variables had strayed outside a narrow range of values for any length of time, life would have been annihilated. (My italics)

They reject as preposterous the notion that this just happened by sheer chance. *Something*, they argue, must have been keeping the planet in its 'just right' condition for those thousands of millions of years. But what?

Gaia, they answer. This is their term, borrowed from the ancient Greeks who had an earth-goddess with that name, for the surface of the planet together with all the living things upon it. The sum total of all this, they reason, must amount to a single living Being – Gaia! And Gaia must possess the marvellous ability to maintain herself in the just-so condition.

Thus atheistic science offers us three explanations why conditions on Planet Earth are suitable for life. You can put it down to an enormously long succession of lucky chances, although more and more scientists seem to be dismissing this idea, because the odds against it are so astronomical.[10]

Or you can believe in an Intelligent Universe.

Or you can believe in an Intelligent Planet.

It is hardly surprising that a great many scientists shake their heads at these scientific 'explanations', and prefer to believe in a Creator God.

Chapter 5

HOW DID LIFE BEGIN?

There is a well-known rule for writers defending the Christian faith, which runs like this: 'Never talk about gaps in scientific knowledge as if they had any connection with a belief in God.' Since I intend to drive a double-decker bus through this rule in the next two chapters, perhaps it would be as well to begin by stating my reasons for doing so.

I do not mean to repeat the blunder made by some authors, who have argued along the following lines:

(1) Science cannot explain such-and-such phenomena.
(2) But we Christians can – we attribute them to the activity of God.
(3) Therefore, as you can't offer any alernative explanation, you ought to accept our explanation and believe in God.

This sort of argument is, quite rightly, rejected by most thinking people. Yet, strange to say, it is frequently dismissed for quite the wrong reasons.

The real reason for rejecting it is that it is a case of what was called the Old Bill syndrome in chapter 3. Your inability to supply a 'better 'ole' is no reason for me to force my own explanation upon you; even if it is the only available one, my explanation could still be a mistake.

But the objections usually raised against that form of argument are on the following lines. First, Christians should see God in *all* natural phenomena, the ones we do understand as well as those we don't – a statement which is true, but not very relevant. Secondly, the gaps in our knowledge are constantly being narrowed, and one day will probably disappear altogether – a statement which is not really true at all.

Those two inadequate reasons were recently stated, yet again, in what is otherwise an excellent little book defending Christianity by a theologian.[1] In support of the second statement he provided a diagram similar to Figure 2. No doubt the average atheist is delighted to see such a picture, as this is just the way he wants Christians to think.

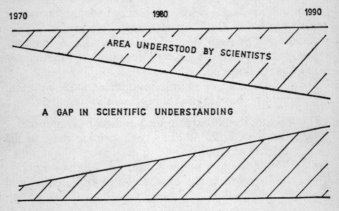

Figure 2. A popular, but false picture of
the situation.

However, only those Christians who have been hoodwinked (and there are many) will accept such a travesty of the situation. Those who have more than a nodding acquaintance with science are aware that Figure 3 is much nearer the truth.

What those gaps really mean

The great Sir Isaac Newton once said that in making his discoveries he felt like a child playing on the seashore; every now and then he was thrilled to find some extra pretty pebble – but all the time a whole ocean of unexplored truth stretched beyond his reach.

72

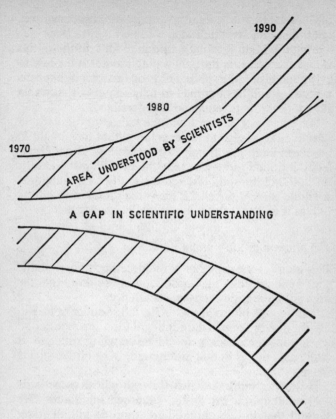

Figure 3. Something more like the real situation.

Nineteenth-century scientists were much less humble. They drew diagrams like Figure 2, and imagined they would soon know all there was to know, or at least everything that was worth knowing.

Modern scientists are more like Newton: they realise that nature is infinitely more complex than Grandad ever dreamed it could be. They are constantly discovering new problems, discovering them faster than they can solve the

73

old problems. For every gap that closes, two new ones open up, as Figure 3 indicates.

My purpose in drawing attention to some of these gaps is quite simple. It is the only way to show that evolutionary humanism, the philosophy of 'evolution explains everything and has put paid to religion', is as shaky as a skyscraper with its foundations undermined.

We must not argue from the existence of gaps in scientific knowledge to the conclusion that men ought to believe in God: that simply does not follow. But it is perfectly legitimate to argue that the evolutionists' case is full of holes, and that consequently the supposed scientific basis of unbelief is ready to crumble away.

This is why those gaps are so vitally important.

The problem of life's origin

This is one of the gaps that have opened up only recently. Two hundred years ago most scientists believed that the origin of life was an everyday occurrence.

Who could blame them? After all, you only had to leave a dish of soup in the cupboard for a few weeks, and when you came back it would be crawling with life. It really did look as if dead matter was giving birth to living things.

It was not until 1862 that the man whose name is on every milkman's lips, Pasteur, exposed this fallacy. He showed that if you sterilised the soup to kill all traces of life, and then kept it free from contamination, no life would appear in it.

Even so, the notion persisted that it couldn't be all that difficult for a bowl of sterile soup to give birth to a primitive organism. Children's books on evolution usually began with a picture of a soupy pool on some primeval seashore, where – presto! – life on earth began. Many a scientist spent countless hours in the laboratory, trying to achieve fame by generating life in a sterile test tube containing nothing but inorganic materials.

Nowadays very few scientists, if any, are sanguine enough to try. They know now what they are up against.

Life, even in its simplest forms, is made of enormously complex molecules. These tower up above the simpler molecules of inorganic (dead) matter like Everest. Today's scientists have to content themselves with taking a few shuffling steps at a time through the foothills.

The simplest living things are microbes. There are two main kinds of these: bacteria, which are relatively large; and viruses, which are much smaller and very much simpler in their structure. In studying the origin of life, scientists naturally focus their attention on the viruses.

Even the smallest of viruses contains hundreds of thousands of atoms. These atoms are joined together to form molecules of two entirely different kinds of chemical: nucleic acid, which may be either DNA (see chapter 2) or its close cousin RNA; and protein.

A typical virus contains one large nucleic acid molecule surrounded by some protein molecules. The life of the virus appears to reside almost entirely in the nucleic acid, and so it is possible to think of a virus as being rather like a miniature snail in a shell of protein.

There are several very important facts to remember about viruses.

(1) Nucleic acid, which is at the heart of every virus, is an extremely complex chemical. The smallest molecule of nucleic acid that has shown the slightest sign of life in the laboratory had more than ten thousand atoms in it, all of which have to be arranged in exactly the right order. And the nucleic acid in the smallest known virus is many times larger than this.

(2) Proteins also are very large and complex molecules.

(3) If you separate the 'snail' of nucleic acid from its 'shell' of protein, it can go into a state resembling hibernation and come to life again when it is recombined with more protein. But the nucleic acid on its own is not a virus; it cannot thrive and multiply without its protein overcoat.

(4) Neither can a complete virus thrive and reproduce itself in a test tube full of chemicals. A virus is a parasite, like a tapeworm; it can only make a living inside the body of some living host, much larger than itself. This is because it lacks the ability to manufacture some elaborate chemicals called enzymes, which it needs in order to grow and reproduce; consequently, it has to live by poaching its host's enzymes.

It all sounds so simple

Bear those four facts in mind while you read the following explanation of how life began, from a recent book by the famous biology professor and science writer Isaac Asimov, who happens to be an unbeliever.

> ... the molecules in the ocean grew gradually more complicated until, eventually, some molecule was somehow formed that could bring about the organisation of simpler molecules into another molecule just like itself. With that, life began and continued, gradually evolving to the present state of affairs . . .[2]

It all sounds so simple, and so plausible – as long as you know nothing about microbiology. But if you have even a rudimentary knowledge of the subject, it is obvious that this explanation is a sorry misrepresentation of modern knowledge.

So far as we know, the only molecules that can reproduce themselves are molecules of nucleic acid. And nucleic acid molecules appear to be incapable of reproducing themselves unless they are inside a living cell, either as an integral part of that cell, or as part of a virus preying on that cell.

We can, if we like, do as Asimov does and speculate that perhaps, under some extraordinary conditions, nucleic acid molecules (or maybe some other sorts of molecules) might be able to reproduce themselves in the absence of other life. But such a suggestion would be little more than a wild, unsupported guess. At the present time all the available evidence points in the opposite direction.

It is difficult to imagine anyone making such a suggestion seriously, except an atheist seeking to justify his position – or an unthinking person parroting that atheist's proposition.

Either way, it really is a remarkable demonstration of the power of prejudice and wishful thinking that a man so knowledgeable as Asimov should go on to say: 'It seems *quite certain*, however, that life developed, not as a miracle but merely because molecules combined with each other along a line of least resistance. Life couldn't help forming . . .'[3] (my italics).

Even that hard-boiled atheist the late Jacques Monod, who, as we saw earlier, has been accused by another unbeliever of being sure about everything, admits it is very difficult to see how a lone molecule could acquire the power of reproduction. The most he allows himself to assert is that, 'This difficulty does not seem insurmountable.'[4]

Quite a number of scientists have concluded that, even if there could be such a thing as a self-reproducing nucleic acid molecule, blind chance alone could never have constructed such an intricate object. Some, like Sir Ernst Chain in the passage quoted on page 40 have concluded that 'directive forces' must have been operating.

Others have speculated along quite different lines. Dr Graham Cairns-Smith, for instance, has spent ten years exploring the possibility that the first living creature might have been a self-reproducing crystal of clay.[5] Most people, however, regard this as even less likely than the usual ideas.

The plain fact is that we have no idea how life began. As one honest biology professor admitted as recently as 1975, 'We can do little more than ask the questions.'[6]

The way chance works

Evolutionists admit that the odds against molecules just 'happening' to come together in such a way as to produce the first living thing are enormous.

But, they add, the universe is a big place and it has been here a long time. Given enough attempts at it, nature was bound to pick a winner sooner or later. In fact, some of them add for good measure, it has probably happened lots of times by now; there may well be life on millions of planets throughout the universe!

This sounds very convincing – until you actually start to do a few sums. Just by way of illustration, it is worth considering what might happen with a box of dice.

If you walked into a casino and found a hundred dice on a table, with every one showing a six, you would say to yourself, 'Ah, somebody has arranged them that way.'

But you could not be quite sure of that. Though very unlikely, it is possible that somebody might have thrown those hundred dice, and by an extraordinary fluke scored six hundred. Obviously, if you throw a set of a hundred dice often enough, six hundred is bound to come up eventually.

Quite true. But have you any idea of how many throws you would be likely to need? If I put down the number it would not mean much, so we will approach the answer another way.

It has been estimated that there are about 1,000,000,000,000,000,000,000 stars in the universe. This might be an underestimate, so I propose to add another three noughts. Further, I am going to suppose that every star has a thousand planets. That gives us a grand total of 1,000,000,000,000,000,000,000,000,000 planets in the universe. (This is certainly a huge overestimate, but never mind. I am in a generous mood today, and what's a few trillion planets between friends, anyway!)

There are about 1,000,000,000 adult men on our own planet. Now let us in our imagination populate each one of our supposed planets with a thousand times as many men as there are on earth – that's 1,000,000,000,000 men per planet – and let's suppose they have been there as long as the universe.

How long is that? The most widely accepted estimate of the age of the universe is 10,000,000,000 years. Again, I shall play for safety and multiply the figure by a hundred.

That leaves us with the following imaginary situation:

1,000,000,000,000,000,000,000,000,000,000 planets.
1,000,000,000,000 men on each planet.
1,000,000,000,000 years they have been there.

And what have all those imaginary men been doing, all that time? Playing with dice, of course!

Each one has a bucket with a hundred dice in it, and because he has had lots of practice he is able to throw them once a second. Ever since the dawn of creation he has been throwing those hundred dice 60 times a minute, 3,600 times an hour, 31 million times a year.

And how many six hundreds have turned up in all that time? None, probably. The odds against *any* of those men *ever* having thrown a six-hundred are still enormous – more than 1,000,000,000,000,000,000 to 1, in fact.[7]

Don't get me wrong. This does not in any way prove that life cannot have originated by chance. It was not intended to. I have a much more limited objective in mind at the moment, but a very important one, none the less. What this rather dicey story proves is this: A highly improbable event still remains a highly improbable event, even when you talk ever so glibly about billions of planets and billions of years.

The chances of life's origin

You may wonder why all this talk about dice. Why don't I get straight down to calculating the odds against life forming on its own?

For a very simple reason. You know exactly where you are with dice, but we don't quite know where we are with atoms and molecules. We do not have enough knowledge to calculate the chances of their joining up in the right way to produce life. Attempts to do this by stalwart defenders of the Christian faith[8] are well meaning but highly inaccurate. Consequently, though their ultimate conclusions may be sound enough, the mathematical arguments on which they base them do not carry much weight.

The trouble is that atoms and molecules are very choosy about their partners. They have strong preferences for joining up with each other in certain ways. When you are studying chance effects in molecules you are, so to speak, playing with loaded dice. And unfortunately we do not know just how heavily the dice are loaded.

What we do know is this. If you prepare a sort of chemical broth, of the kind that might have existed in muddy pools when Earth was young, and bombard it with radiation, quite a number of sizeable molecules are formed[9] – far more than would happen if the small molecules of the basic chemicals were just lumped together in a haphazard way. Obviously, the dice are loaded quite a lot.

Nevertheless, the dice are not loaded nearly as much as the atheists could wish. Such experiments produce only fair-sized molecules: they do not come within a hundred miles of producing the huge molecules needed to sustain life. The odds against these being formed are undoubtedly enormous, but nobody can say just how enormous.

One thing is certain, however. We know the chemistry of nucleic acid is such that it cannot grow and multiply without the help of some other extremely complex molecules called enzymes.[10] And any old enzyme will not do; there are millions of different enzymes and nearly all of them are good trade unionists – they each do a different job, and are most reluctant to do another enzyme's job for it.[11]

Consequently, all the available evidence says that the first nucleic acid molecule would have got nowhere on its own. It could not have reproduced itself until the right enzyme (or enzymes, for it would almost certainly have needed more than one) had been formed in quantity, right next door to it. It is almost laughable the way popular science writers ignore this fact, with their romantic tales of, 'Abracadabra! The first living molecule was born.'

Biochemists are well aware of the difficulty, of course, and have spent a great deal of effort searching for a solution. A number of textbooks on the problem of life's origin have been published in recent years,[12] but the main purpose they serve is to show how enormously complicated the whole subject is, and how science is still quite incapable of explaining it.

By and large, the serious textbooks are much more honest about the difficulties than the popular science writers. One such book published in 1974[13] begins: 'It must be admitted from the beginning that we do not know how life began ... we do not yet have one plausible, detailed and complete hypothesis [of life's origin].'

This is a fair statement of the position – not by a creationist, but by two authors who believe that life arose from dead matter. And they freely admit that not only are they and their colleagues short of facts – they don't even have one decent *theory* as yet!

Returning to the subject of enzymes, the odds against the right ones being formed in the right place at the right time are even more tremendous than the odds against the formation of the first living molecule itself. As a standard textbook on enzymes admits: 'The whole subject of the origin of enzymes ... bristles with difficulties. We may surely say of the origin of enzymes, as Hopkins said of the advent of life, that it was "the most improbable and the most significant event in the history of the universe".[14] Clearly, the combined odds against a living nucleic acid molecule being formed by chance, *and* the necessary enzymes for it being formed alongside it, are so fantastic that it is just not on – no matter how big or how old the universe may be.[15]

Of course, there is always another possibility. Maybe there is some other sort of giant molecule, all unknown to science, that is capable of confounding all the laws of biochemistry as we know them, by living and growing and reproducing without the aid of enzymes.

Yes, maybe there is. Maybe there are Loch Ness Monsters, and flying saucers, and Fairy Queens, too. But until somebody produces some specimens there can be no sense in taking any of those possibilities very seriously in a scientific discussion.

At the present time there is far more reason to believe in a Creator than in the mythical Magic Molecule.

The first living cell

The next great mystery of biology is how the first cell arose. There is a tremendous gap between viruses and the simplest one-celled creatures, such as bacteria, and no one knows how it was bridged.

The essential difference is that a bacterium is self-supporting. A virus has to make do with the enzymes it can steal from its host, but bacteria make their own enzymes, which in turn help to make other vital chemicals. Thus the humble bacterium carries around with it as many life-support systems as a spaceship.

All this complex chemical apparatus is sealed inside a very special kind of wall. This acts as a sort of selective filter: it lets in those chemicals which the bacterium needs, but prevents the vitally important enzymes from escaping.

82

The heart of the bacterium is, of course, nucleic acid, which is at the centre of all life. But whereas a simple virus has only one kind, a bacterium contains many different kinds of nucleic acid.

Each of these varieties of nucleic acid can make one particular enzyme. The many different enzymes in the bacterium do many jobs: in particular, they manufacture the material for the cell wall, and they enable the nucleic acids to reproduce themselves. All this strenuous activity enables bacteria to grow and multiply at a fearful rate when conditions are favourable for it, as we all know to our cost when we pick up an infection.

However simple it may have been, the very first bacterium must have had at least those three components, working together as a team: nucleic acids, enzymes, and a cell wall. The problem is, which came first – the chicken, the egg, or the hen-coop?

Nucleic acid cannot be formed without the aid of enzymes. Some enzymes can only be manufactured by other enzymes, and these other enzymes can only be manufactured by nucleic acid. Cell walls are only made by enzymes. And the enzymes cannot do their job unless they are kept in place by the cell wall.

So how on earth did it all start?

Even the near-omniscient Monod cannot answer that question. He admits:

The development of the metabolic system [in the first cells] ... poses Herculean problems. So does the emergence of the selectively permeable membrane [the cell wall] without which there can be no viable cell. But the major problem is the origin of the genetic code and of its translation mechanism [that is, of each particular nucleic acid's ability to manufacture one particular enzyme]. *Indeed, it is not so much a 'problem' as a veritable enigma.*[16] (My italics)

83

Looking for an explanation

Much research has been done on this problem, but with very little to show for it. Fifty years ago a Russian biologist[17] made the most useful suggestion yet. He pointed out that in the right kind of chemical broth, large molecules would cluster together like a swarm of bees. Perhaps bunches of molecules like this somehow turned into the first living cell.

Others have followed up this lead. Molecule clusters have been studied at great length. They have been observed to change their shape and their size, to split up and come together again – but they remain nothing more nor less than molecule clusters.

They have nothing to tell us about how the first cell can have formed. You might as well try to learn how a bunch of grapes grows by playing with a box of billiard balls. Like every other approach to the problem, this avenue is a dead end.

So what we have is not so much a gap as a Grand Canyon. In Act I, Scene 1 of the great Drama of Life we have nothing but magic molecules foraging for their food in the primitive ocean. In Scene 2 we have a complicated piece of biological machinery, with all its parts working together in perfect harmony, each quite incapable of existing apart from the whole.

What happened between the two scenes? How did Life manage to leap across the enormous chasm between the virus-like living molecule and the bacterium-like simple cell?

If you ask a well-informed and frank-speaking biologist this question, he would probably answer something like this: 'We don't know. It will be a long, long time before we do know – if ever we do. All we can be sure of is that the gap was crossed, or we should not be here. Since we reject the idea of a Creator at work, we can only accept that life must have struggled across the gap on its own, somehow.'

So here we are again, back at the same old brick wall. The evidence stares us in the face that the simplest living cell is an assembled mechanism, an artefact, a created thing. But most biologists nowadays look at the evidence with blinkers on their eyes, blinkers labelled, 'There is no God.' So do many other people.

Is it surprising that they cannot recognise His handiwork when it is placed in front of them?

Chapter 6

GAPS GALORE

My first experiment in aerodynamics was carried out at
the age of about ten. Like many another small boy I was
fascinated by the idea of flight, and wanted to see how a
parachute worked. So I jumped off the roof of a large
shed, hopefully clutching an umbrella. To my disgust the
brolly had no noticeable effect on my speed of descent
and I suffered a severe shake-up, although mercifully no
bones were broken. The lesson lasted me a long time.

When I grew older I learnt that parachutes may look
like umbrellas but are, in fact, many times larger. There is
a simple reason for this. Because air is an extremely 'thin'
substance (of low density, to use the scientific term) its
lifting power is very small indeed, and it takes an extremely large area of fabric to support the weight of a
man.

Flying, in fact, is very much harder than it looks. Long
before Wilbur and Orville Wright made the first powered
flight, lots of men had learnt this the hard way, injuring
or killing themselves in attempts to imitate the birds.

All these early efforts to fly failed because they depended upon human muscle power, and this simply is not
sufficient for the purpose. In a lightweight structure with
a very large area of wing – in other words, a glider – a
man can float gently down to the ground, or, if he is lucky
enough to find an up-current, he may manage to drift
about in the air for a long time before at last he is forced
down. But despite an enormous amount of research, man
has not yet invented a device that will enable him to take
off and fly a worthwhile distance in still air without the
help of an aero engine.

How did birds manage it?

According to the theory of evolution, birds are descended from animals of some sort, probably from reptiles. But how did they first acquire the ability to take off? This is a question which evolutionists generally try to sweep under the carpet.

The problem is that evolution can only have occurred in small steps. The idea that a chance mutation could ever have caused a reptile to lay an egg with a bird in it is laughable – so laughable that even the most hardened evolutionists scoff at it. As one popular book on evolution admits, 'It is inconceivable that the flight feathers of a bird could have arisen by a single mutation.'[1]

What, then, is the alternative? If feathers, and the astonishingly lightweight wing structures of birds, and their tremendously powerful wing muscles – all three of which are equally essential for flight – evolved in a long succession of small steps, how did this occur?

Evolution declares that the only mutations able to survive are those which benefit the creature concerned. But what use is a partly formed feather, or a partly formed wing? They would only be a nuisance, an encumbrance, a positive handicap in the fight for survival. (If you can't appreciate the difficulty, just imagine yourself trying to survive in the jungle with half a parachute or half a hang-glider permanently attached!)

The way evolutionists gloss over this problem is almost unbelievable. As recently as 1976 one of them was still contending in a learned journal[2] that the first stumpy feathers on one of the earliest birds would have helped it to glide away from its pursuers.

By arguing like this he was greatly overestimating the lifting power of the air on small surfaces – just as I did long ago in my umbrella exploit. This was perhaps an understandable mistake for a small boy to make, but not what one expects from an intelligent scientist.

Most evolutionists realise the absurdity of this

approach. Yet the alternatives they offer are just as ridiculous. Some argue that feathers first evolved as quilts for keeping birds warm, and only afterwards were found useful for flying.[3] But this cannot be, because the kind of downy feathers that keep heat in, which occur on adult birds' breasts and all over young chicks, are quite different from wing feathers. And what about the lightweight wing structure, and the highly specialised, powerful wing wing muscles, without which the best of feathers would be useless?

Other evolutionists[4] reason that the first feathers evolved as devices for capturing small prey. Then, one day, some lucky possessor of this new insect-trap found that if he swung it hard enough he became airborne!

Of course, anybody who has ever used a butterfly-net is well aware that it only works because it slips through the air with very little resistance – whereas wings work by producing a *maximum* of air resistance. But evolutionists are made of stern stuff, and are not deterred by little difficulties like that.

The birds, the bats and the bees

The origin of flight in birds is not an isolated problem. According to evolutionists, the ability to fly evolved on at least three separate occasions. Birds solved the problem in one way, bats in another, and insects in another.

In some ways insect flight is the most marvellous of all. It takes so much energy for a honeybee to fly that its temperature rises by more than fifteen degrees during flight.[5] An insect's wings would be useless appendages without the marvellous mini-motor that drives them. But even a bee's remarkable power-pack cannot help it to fly if an accident (or a heartless experimenter) chops off the ends of its wings.

With insects, birds and bats alike, flying is an all-or-

88

nothing affair. Anything less than a complete set of flying equipment is worse than useless, a hindrance to survival rather than a help.

Evolutionists are – almost literally – at their wits' end trying to explain each of the three separate flight problems. There is no shortage of explanations; the only trouble is that they are all so wildly improbable.

Now and again an unusually honest evolutionist will admit this. In 1973, for instance, Sir Vincent Wigglesworth wrote a major paper on the origin of insect flight in which he concluded: 'I claim, therefore, that the dispersal theory of the origin of insect flight, most of the elements of which have been put forward at one time or another during the past hundred years, *offers the least strain to the imagination*'[6] (my italics).

This is a fine recommendation for a scientific theory – that it offers rather less strain to the imagination than its competitors! Here is the Old Bill syndrome raging unchecked, as it so often does in evolutionary theory.

The plain fact is that no one has yet explained how flight could possibly have evolved without some creative Power at work. The odds against it happening once are absolutely enormous; the evolutionists' claim that it must have occurred three times is even more unbelievable than a punter's tale that he has won half-million pound prizes on the pools three weeks running.

As if to add insult to intellectual injury, a biologist is liable to retort, 'That's not such a dreadful problem. It is simply an example of parallel evolution.'

Parallel evolution, indeed. This is just another example of a famous fallacy which crops up in every branch of science – the notion that giving a high-sounding name to a problem is a way of explaining it. The truth is that 'parallel evolution' merely describes the difficulty that evolutionists are facing: it does not take them one inch nearer to a solution.

Why kangaroos hop

That curious-looking animal, the kangaroo, has always baffled people. The early settlers in Australia could hardly believe their eyes when these ungainly creatures hopped away faster than many a horse could gallop. How on earth could any hopping creature keep up a steady twenty-five miles an hour for miles on end, and belt along at forty for short stretches?

Recent research at Harvard[7] has at last pulled the kangaroo's secret out of the pouch. A kangaroo's undercarriage is built like an ingenious system of springs, in which its huge tail plays a major part. It is nature's equivalent of the pogo stick. But it only works well at high speeds. If a kangaroo wants to travel slowly it lumbers along on all four feet. When danger threatens, the front feet are lifted clear of the ground and kanga hops it. And the Harvard researchers, using elaborate measuring techniques, found that the faster the kangaroo hops the more efficient this method of travel becomes.

In the light of these discoveries, evolutionists are faced with difficulties abounding. The kangaroo's hopping-gear is another all-or-nothing system. It is no use at all to its proprietor until it is sufficiently well formed to operate efficiently at high speeds. A half-evolved kangaroo-kit would only be a drag on its owner. Two short legs plus two long legs plus an awkward great tail would be a perfect recipe for extinction – unless and until they housed an effective hopping outfit.

What, then, caused the kangaroo's brilliantly successful method of travel to evolve? It certainly could not have been natural selection, which would surely have wiped out kanga's earliest ancestors.

Another unorthodox animal

Another of nature's comedians is the camel – a sort of horse that has been designed by a committee, as a frustrated chairman once described it.

The camel can well afford to turn up its supercilious nose at us. Ugly-looking brute though it may be, it can survive in a waterless desert many times longer than we can. How does it manage it?

Research has shown that the camel has not one secret of survival, but several.[8] These are the principal ones:

(1) A camel can lose a quarter of its weight by evaporation of water from its tissues without suffering any harm. Very little of this water comes from its blood. By contrast, when we go thirsty we soon start losing water from our bloodstream; long before we have lost anything like a quarter of our own weight of water our blood becomes so thick that we die.

(2) A camel's urine is very much more concentrated than a man's. Consequently it can get rid of waste products without using nearly as much water as we do.

(3) Our bodies need to stay at a constant temperature. In the desert we have to sweat furiously to keep our temperatures somewhere near the usual 98.4° F. A camel doesn't bother. He lets his huge body cool down to 93° at night and then warm up again gradually to 105° by day; that way he doesn't need to start sweating until late in the day when he reaches the 105° mark.

(4) A man's body is covered with a layer of fat, which keeps the heat in, while his sweat glands are *outside* this insulating layer, and so are not very efficient at cooling him. A camel, however, has no covering layer of fat to keep the heat *in*; it is covered with hair which keeps the heat *out*, while its sweat glands are *inside* this insulating layer and consequently work very efficiently.

(5) Ever wondered what those humps were for? That's why the camel is not kept warm, as we are, by a coating of fat – the camel's fat is stored in the most efficient way possible, in one or two large lumps.

How did it come about?

The question is: did this remarkable collection of properties come together by chance, through a series of
evolutionary processes? Or is it more likely to be the
work of a purposeful Creator, deliberately fashioning a
creature for desert-dwelling man to use?

If evolution is the answer, then why did the camel
adopt so many different devices for conserving water?
Having evolved two or three of them, and thus gained the
edge over its competitors, what incentive did it have to
evolve any more water-saving mechanisms? And why
did other desert species not follow the camel's example?
There are thousands of such species; why aren't they all
fitted with camel-hair coats and humps?

As a matter of fact it is not nearly so easy to evolve the
ability to tolerate the desert as might be expected. Bedouin Arabs have been living there for thousands of years,
and although nobody expected them to have evolved
humps, evolutionists once thought that the Bedouin
might at least have developed the ability, say, to pass
concentrated urine.

Alas, it is not so. Extensive research has now shown
that after thousands of years occupancy, those Sons of
the Desert are no better equipped by nature to live there
than anybody else.[9]

The riddle of instinct

Man is now able to build such remarkable machines that
he likes to call them 'electronic brains'. An automatic
pilot can fly an airliner, which is something that most of
us can't do. A large computer can keep track of the bank
accounts of a million people, which is more than any
human being can manage.

Yet these remarkable inventions are not intelligent.
They may appear to be clever, but in reality they are

quite incapable of rational thought. They only do what their human creators programme them to do.

There is a counterpart to this in the animal world, which we call instinct. A spider is programmed to spin a web; a bird is programmed to build a nest; a butterfly is programmed to lay its eggs on a particular kind of leaf, so that its grubs will hatch out with the right food at hand. And so on, almost endlessly, throughout the animal world.

Where did all these instincts come from? Were they programmed into the creatures concerned by some supernatural Programmer? Or did they just evolve by natural processes?

It may be difficult for many people to accept the first answer, because it means believing in God. But to accept the second answer is not just difficult: it is practically impossible, unless we are prepared to sweep aside the facts.

Take the strange behaviour of the Australian mallee fowl, *Leipoa ocellata*,[10] sometimes called the incubator bird. The male is a powerful creature, and at nesting time his built-in programme moves him to find a patch of sandy soil where he can excavate a pit about three feet deep and ten or twelve feet across. He then proceeds to drag vegetation into the hole until it is more than brim full. After that he waits until rain has saturated the contents of the pit, and then covers it with a thick layer of sand, ending up with a huge mound perhaps fifteen feet in diameter and five feet high – and all this just to provide his mate with a self-incubating nest!

As every gardener knows, a compost heap gets warm as it rots. But just 'warm' is not good enough for the male incubator bird. His mate's eggs need a constant temperature of approximately 92°, and he is programmed to ensure that they get it. Several times a day he uses his beak as a thermometer to probe the heap. If the temperature is too high he makes ventilation holes to cool things down; too low, and he adds another blanket of sand. When the temperature is just right he permits the hen to lay her eggs in the compost, but until then he compels her to wait.

In the autumn there is less sap in the vegetation, and consequently the mallee fowl's compost heap ferments more slowly and generates less heat. But the incubator bird's instinct tells it how to deal with that situation. Each autumn morning he removes sand from the top of the heap to allow the eggs to be warmed by the sun; and late in the afternoon he puts it all back again, to conserve heat during the night.

Biologists know that this bird's astonishing behaviour is programmed in its nucleic acid molecules, but they cannot tell how it got there. To say, 'It must have evolved', is delightfully easy, but to explain how it could possibly have done so is another matter.

Like the wing of a bird, like a computer program, the incubator bird's strange instinct is an all-or-nothing affair. Until the instinct was fully formed it must have been a dead loss to the bird that possessed it. That being so, how could it possibly have evolved in the series of small steps that evolutionary theory demands?

And in any case, what incentive could there be for an evolving species to give up hatching eggs in the usual way and adopt this complicated procedure instead?

Biologists have no answer. Some of them realise that the incubator bird's incredible skill is most likely to have been planted in it by some great creative Power. Others refuse to admit this – but they are quite unable to offer any reasonable alternative.

The miracle of migration

One of the most remarkable forms of instinct is the power to navigate. Migrating creatures possess this ability to an extraordinary degree. As recently as World War II, ships and aircraft could not navigate anything like as well as many living creatures.

Biologists recognise two distinct problems here. First,

there is the comparatively easy one: how do they do it? Even this has been only partially answered.

Birds make use of the stars on the early stages of their journey – provided, of course, that the stars are shining. Some species seem to possess a kind of natural compass, with which they can somehow sense the direction of the earth's magnetic field. How they find their way when they approach the end of their journey is a mystery: all we know is that somehow many birds manage to travel thousands of miles and find the very nest they left the year before.

Then there are fish like the salmon, which can cross a whole ocean and return unerringly to the self-same stream where it was spawned. Perhaps they go by the taste and the smell of the water around them, or the particular pattern made by the throbbing of the waves; nobody knows for sure.

Some sea animals are almost as brilliant. Every year the grey whale travels from the Arctic Ocean to tropical Mexico, to mate in the same narrow-mouthed lagoon. The fur seal travels much the same route in reverse; he goes from California each year to the Arctic, to mate in the tiny Pribilof Islands.

This brings us to the really difficult question. Did this superb navigational instinct evolve? Because if so, how? It's another form of the same old problem that keeps cropping up – what use is a half-developed ability to navigate? About as much good as a compass with no needle!

But that is not all. Let us suppose that one day some imaginative genius will conjure up a faintly plausible explanation of how this instinct might just possibly have evolved in stages. Immediately he would find himself up against another problem.

In one human lifetime the stars all remain in the same part of the sky. That is why we call them the 'fixed' stars, as opposed to the planets which move in their orbits. We can steer very easily by the Pole Star because as long as anyone can remember it has sat right over the North Pole.

Yet ten thousand years ago, what we know as the Pole Star was in quite a different part of the sky. And ten thousand years is only a fleeting moment, compared with the time-scale of evolution. Consequently, if birds gradually evolved their ability to steer by the stars, they must have done it over a period when the stars were wandering all over the sky.

The same difficulty arises with all the other supposed methods of finding the way home. Over the past few thousand years the earth's magnetic field has pointed all ways, and the salt composition of our coastal waters has been continually changing. How could any species first acquire the ability to navigate when all its navigational aids were drifting about? Anybody can use a moving navigational beacon once he has become an expert navigator, of course – but imagine trying to teach yourself the rudiments of navigation while all the available beacons were on the move!

Finally, it should be noted that this near-impossible feat had to be accomplished not once but at least three times. If evolution really is the answer, then the navigational instinct must have evolved once in birds, and again in mammals, and yet again in fishes.

Well, where does the truth really lie? Was this extraordinary power evolved, in some manner that no one can even begin to explain? Or did some greater Power create it? Which seems more likely?

The tale of a tail

Ever since Darwin's day biologists have been arguing about peacocks' tails.

For someone who believes in a Creator who likes creating beautiful things, there is no problem. But Darwin saw things differently. To him, organs developed as a consequence of the struggle for survival. Therefore, he reasoned, its tail must somehow help a peacock to survive.

But how? What practical use could a great big, beautiful tail be to any bird? It can only hinder his chances of survival by slowing him down.

Darwin eventually solved the problem to his own satisfaction. His highly ingenious explanation ran something like this:

'Let's suppose that, in the days before peacocks started to evolve, there was a species of bird where all the hens had an eye for beauty. One day a mutation occurred, and a lot of cocks were hatched out with long tails. Needless to say, these hindered them from getting about, and more than usual of these long-tailed cocks were eaten by their enemies, while the short-tailed variety survived as well as ever.

'But there was another side to the situation. The hens were so infatuated with the survivors among these long-tailed heroes that they were reluctant to mate with the short-tailed cocks. Surviving is no use to you in the long run if you can't find a mate; so the hens had mostly long-tailed offspring, and the shorties eventually died out.'

The same sort of argument is used to explain a great many beautiful but useless appendages in all kinds of living creatures. It is also applied to what you might call beautiful but useless *behaviour* – namely, the elaborate courtship dances performed by so many species.

For various reasons many biologists reject Darwin's bright idea. For one thing, the kind of female choosiness that he thought was common has not been proved to occur in nature at all.[11] For another, it seems most unlikely that the enormous handicap to survival imposed by a long, unwieldy tail could be offset by a mere improvement in one's chances in the marriage market.

Every so often a biologist produces an alternative explanation, but without any lasting success. For instance, Zahavi published a brilliant new theory in 1975 – only to be shot down in flames by several other biologists in 1976.[12]

Thus the problem that worried Darwin is still unsolved today. Evolutionary theory is still unable to account for the existence of beauty in nature. The only satisfactory explanation of it has stood for three thousand years:

> Lord, you have made so many things!
> How wisely you made them all!
> The earth is filled with your creatures.[13]

Some other problems

I have rationed myself to this one chapter for pointing out the weaknesses of Darwinism. This has meant being highly selective with the available material, and so I have concentrated on those topics where most readers will feel at home.

Now, for the sake of any biologists who may read this book, I must mention briefly a few points of a slightly more technical nature. So long as problems like these remain unsolved, surely evolution cannot be regarded as any more than a theory awaiting either confirmation or disproof.

(1) *The Cambrian explosion*

At the start of the Cambrian era, about 600 million years ago, an extraordinary series of events occurred. Before it there seems to have been no life except for microscopic single cells, and perhaps a few small, soft-bodied creatures like worms and jellyfish. After it, the world was filled with a huge variety of living things. The change was so rapid, and the results so grand, that it is often called the Cambrian 'explosion'.

If this was not the result of a great outburst of activity by a Creator, then what caused it? And why has nothing like it ever happened since?

Nobody can say. As one writer on the subject commented, 'An enormous variety of hypotheses have been advanced'[14] – but none of them is convincing.

(2) *Goldschmidt's unsolved problems*
Professor R. B. Goldschmidt was an evolutionist of international renown, but not of the usual starry-eyed variety. His book on evolution[15] pointed out that the theory was still full of holes.

He listed a great many features of plant and animal life that evolutionary theory cannot explain. They are all things that simply cannot have evolved on a step-by-step basis. Like most of the examples earlier in this chapter, they are in the 'all-or-nothing' class.

Many of Goldschmidt's problems relate to the nitty gritty of biology and are not suitable for discussion here. Some of them are easy to appreciate, and among these is the poison apparatus of snakes.

This deadly weapon has to include: (1) a chemical plant for making the venom, (2) a safe storage vessel for it, (3) an elaborate delivery system (fangs), (4) the instinctive skill to use the weapon effectively, (5) safeguards to ensure that the snake does not poison itself. How did that little lot evolve in stages? It is pointless merely to tickle one's prey: a snake's poison-pack is useless unless it is powerful enough to kill or disable.

Most of the problems in Goldschmidt's long list are equally tricky. This is why, nearly forty years after publication, few of them are any nearer solution.

Very few of today's dedicated evolutionists have read Goldschmidt. They are too closely akin to the medieval priests who refused to look through Galileo's telescope for fear that they might have to alter their views.

(3) *Gaps between species*
Darwin's bombshell was called *The Origin of Species* for a good reason. Previously, people had thought that the lines of division between species were clearcut, and could never be crossed.

Darwin showed that this was not so. Occasionally different species in the wild can interbreed and have fertile offspring. This being so, perhaps all species of living things share a common ancestor, reasoned Darwin.

But although the gaps between species are not quite as clearcut as creationists often make out, they are still a great deal bigger than evolutionists could wish. Human selection is much more effective than natural selection, and yet deliberate selection has never produced a new species. Dog breeders can produce only dogs, rose breeders nothing but roses. Even those ardent experimenters the fruit-fly breeders, who run through dozens of generations in a year, have never bred anything but weird, misshapen fruit flies.

Many evolutionists are frankly embarrassed by these facts. A recent book on evolution[16] began by admitting that species 'tend to persist virtually the same for generation after generation'.

Another evolutionist, reviewing the book, made this comment on the statement quoted above: 'True, but not an idea I would choose to emphasise at the start of a book on evolution.'[17]

That last remark is very revealing. Evidently it is rank bad manners to let the cat out of the bag in evolutionary circles.

(4) *Gaps in the fossil record*

Darwin was not greatly worried about missing links in his evolutionary chain. Fossil-hunting was in its infancy in his day, and he could argue, without being unreasonable, 'Just give it time. All those missing fossils will no doubt turn up.'

Well, we have given it time – more than a hundred years, in fact. A vast army of paleontologists (fossil experts) has been burrowing away, and what is the result? Let two of them speak for themselves:

There is no need to apologise any longer for the poverty of the fossil record. In some ways it has become almost unmanageably rich ... *The fossil record nevertheless continues to be composed mainly of gaps.*[18] (My italics)

It remains true, as every paleontologist knows, that most new species, genera and families, and nearly all categories above the level of families, *appear in the record suddenly* and are not led up to by known, gradual, completely continuous transitional sequences.[19] (My italics)

If evolutionary theory were half as soundly based as it is made out to be, many of those gaps ought to have been filled by now. But they have not been.[20]

A double challenge

A few years ago, the scientific journal *Nature* had a brilliant but unconventional editor, John Maddox. In 1972 he took a daring step and opened his correspondence columns to critics of evolution. This was probably the first time in history that biology's sacred cow was exposed so freely to attack.

Believers in creation took full advantage of their opportunity, and a selection of their letters was published. Editors can't stand long letters, and so they were compelled to make their points very brief. This led to a stinging reply from one dedicated evolutionist, who wrote: 'A number of creationists have written vaguely of "flaws" and "unanswered questions" in evolutionary thought. Such as? Even if there are any, this alone is not enough: creationism must be seen to be a better fit to the data.'[21] (Those last few words are ambiguous, but he undoubtedly means, 'it is up to creationists to show that creationism is a better fit to the data.')

This correspondent's phrase, 'even if there are any', is a delicious example of the head-in-a-sack outlook of many biologists. We have seen in this chapter that there

101

are lots and lots and lots of them, and every biologist worth his salt ought to be well aware of this. Yet, sadly, many of them are blind to the facts.

In effect, this evolutionist posed a double challenge to those who believe in creation: (1) show me any flaws in the wonderful theory of evolution, (2) prove that creationism is 'a better fit to the data'.

His first challenge was naive, and has been amply answered in this chapter. But his other challenge is a much more serious one. Is there really any *positive* evidence for a Creator?

Yes, there is – a great deal of it, in fact. The rest of this book will be devoted to it. But as you read on, don't forget what has gone before. Beware of slipping back unconsciously into taking evolution for granted.

We have seen ample evidence that evolution is nothing more than a speculative theory, with plenty of evidence appearing to support it, but a great deal of evidence against it, too.

Evolution has neither been proved nor disproved yet. It is still on trial, and is likely to remain so for a long time to come. Do not allow an unproved theory to blind your mind to the evidence which will follow.

Chapter 7

DOES NATURE KNOW WHERE IT IS GOING?

Go into the streets of any of our big cities around ten o'clock at night, and you will see two different kinds of dogs. Some are being taken for their ritual evening walk by their devoted owners; others have just been shooed out of the house for a few minutes, to fend for themselves.

The difference between them is striking. The loners just mooch around from one sniffing-point to another. Obviously bored, they don't see any point in going anywhere, so they hang about within whistling distance of home and wait for the call to come in. They look only half alive by contrast with the other lucky dogs.

As every dog knows, having your master with you makes all the difference. You may not know *where* you are being taken, but you know that you *are* being taken, and that's enough to fill your doggy heart with a joyous sense of anticipation.

When you are allowed off the lead you will sometimes lag behind and sometimes race ahead or dodge from side to side. Because of this you will cover three miles for every mile your master walks. But you will never be more than fifty yards from his heels, so that by and large your route will be the same as his. You scamper along happily because the presence of your master has instilled a measure of direction into your evening exercises.

Even a dog, it seems, likes to have a sense of purpose in life. And, as we shall see shortly, it rather looks as if Mother Nature does, too.

Movement in one direction

As we saw in chapter 2, the fossils in the rocks tell us a great deal about the history of life on earth, over the past thousand million years or so.

First, there was nothing but single-celled creatures like bacteria.[1] Then came a great variety of lowly creatures of the sea: sponges, jellyfish, worms, shellfish, water weeds, and the like. Later, fish appeared with fins so that they could go where they pleased; then land creatures with legs, and birds with wings; plants covered the land, and eventually huge trees sprang up; animals with bigger and bigger brains were formed – and eventually our own race came along.

This account of life's history, of course, is very much old hat. We are all so familiar with it that most of us can see nothing to get excited about.

And that is exactly where we slip up. Because that sequence of events is really one of the most astonishing things in this astonishing world of ours!

Why should the story of living things be one long story of steady progress, from bacteria, all the way up the ladder of life, to man? Evolutionists have no answer to that question, except to say, in very skilful language, well dressed with mathematics, 'That's the way it happened.'[2]

Some prominent biologists are obviously uncomfortable with the question. They can see all too clearly where it is leading. So they declare that there has not been any 'progress' in the ordinary sense of the word – just 'change', which looks to us like progress because we happen to prefer men to bacteria.

Such arguments lack conviction, however, even with the majority of biologists. Most of them still insist on talking about 'higher' and 'lower' forms of life; thus they recognise that life really has moved in one direction – upwards. And that is another way of saying it has made progress.

Yet if the course of life depended on blind chance, it

ought to have wandered about aimlessly like a dog left to itself, never moving far from its starting point. Mutations can take life downhill just as easily as uphill. So can natural selection: if the drying up of seas caused fins to evolve into legs, the flooding of continents could equally well cause legs to evolve back into fins.

It can be argued that 'backward progress' has sometimes occurred. For example, a few birds, like the ostrich, have lost the ability to fly. And an enormous number of prehistoric animals and plants have become extinct.

True. But these are only minor wobbles in the path of life's progress, which, if you take an overall view, has been advancing continuously.

The progress of life is, in point of fact, very similar to that of the dog being taken for a walk. He frequently zig-zags; he occasionally back-tracks; he explores every blind alley that he comes across. But all these wanderings are only incidentals. The one really important fact is that, by and large, the dog follows the path his master maps out for him.

Thus it has been with Mother Nature during the past thousand million years or so. She hasn't followed an absolutely straight course. She has made her zig-zags and back-tracks, and what with mammoths and dinosaurs and the rest she has explored countless dead ends. But none of this can alter the fact that she has travelled a long, long road in one direction.

Are we going to say that nobody directed nature in this one direction – that all this progress is the result of chance encounters of atoms and molecules? Surely not. Surely it is a 'better fit to the data' to reason that nature in her long walk was following her Master's footsteps.

Playing with fire

One of the great differences between man and the animals is that man can plan for the future while animals cannot. Squirrels, of course, store up nuts for the winter and bees gather honey, but planning does not enter into such operations. Every cell in a squirrel's body carries a piece of nucleic acid with a program written into it: 'Store up nuts!' The squirrel unthinkingly does what this instinct tells him.

Man's forward planning is altogether different. He can set himself a long-term objective and work out a way to achieve it. On the way he may endure all sorts of discomforts for the sake of his distant goal.

Some of the early workers with dangerous chemicals, for instance, were killed or injured when their apparatus exploded. The survivors pressed on with the risky work, believing that one day the results would benefit humanity or win for themselves fame and fortune. They played with fire because they knew where they were going; they trusted that one day they or their children would benefit.

There are a number of instances where nature has played with fire, either literally or figuratively. Perhaps the most spectacular case is that of the bombardier beetle who actually repels his enemies with what practically amounts to a flamethrower, like some mythical dragon come to life. He does it by using two dangerous chemicals which, when brought together in the presence of suitable catalysts, will explode – a technique well known to the IRA and their like.

The explosive chemicals (hydroquinone and hydrogen peroxide) are manufactured in separate glands and stored in separate vessels. The catalyst consists of a mixture of two very different enzymes, each of which has a particular property that makes the mixture a perfect detonator for the beetle's explosive.

At the rear of the beetle's body is a combustion chamber, suitably lined with material resembling asbestos, and an opening which can be aimed at the enemy. When he sees the whites of their eyes, the bombardier beetle injects his two explosive chemicals and his enzyme mixture into the combustion chamber, and – pouff! – the body of a scorched predator falls to the ground.

It is no wonder that an eminent German scientist who has studied its strange chemistry has written, 'Such an explosion in a living organism would be inconceivable with any biochemical system other than that of the bombardier beetle.'[3]

This extraordinary device is a wonderful aid to survival *now that it is perfected*. But if it was produced by the blind trial-and-error method of evolution, what horrors the earlier generations of beetles must have endured for the sake of posterity!

Anybody who has ever worked in a research laboratory will have no difficulty in visualising a stern-faced Mother Nature, addressing the grief-stricken survivors of one of the earlier, unsuccessful experiments:

'Never mind, lads. It's worth pressing on. This is going to be the ultimate weapon. When we've got it perfected it will make you the masters of the insect world. Let's try again. We shall need to change the formula of Ingredient A, increase the injection rate of B to give more thorough mixing, improve the detonator, and widen the flame orifice to keep the blast pressures down – oh, yes, and we'll thicken up the walls of the combustion chamber to give you more protection. I'm sure we shan't lose so many of you in the next set of trials.'

Seriously, though, isn't it obvious that natural forces alone could never have produced a bombardier beetle? Natural selection would very soon have exterminated the first beetles to start playing with fire, long before the beetles' weapons became an aid to survival. Nature would have had to have known where she was going, and to have been determined to get there whatever the cost, when she first started fitting flamethrowers into beetles.

And since nature is not an intelligent being, and consequently has no sense of purpose, there must be Somebody behind nature who designed and built the strange weaponry of the bombardier beetle.

Some other risky devices

In the more usual figurative sense of the expression, nature seems to love playing with fire. And she has done it with great success. Even Lucretia Borgia never mastered the trick of eating snakes and swallowing the nutritious parts while keeping the poison fangs safely tucked under her lip, so that she could subsequently kiss her enemies to death. Yet some living creatures make their living by stunts like that.

One of them is the larva of an insect called the North American conifer sawfly.[4] Its staple diet is pine needles. These are packed with sticky resins which may smell fragrant to us but are deadly poison to insects.

But this does not worry the sawfly. When he munches a pine needle he carefully extracts the poisonous goo and puts it away in a couple of sacs at the side of his head; then he swallows the digestible part with as much satisfaction as a man who has just managed to pull all the bones out of a kipper.

You might think that he would throw away the poisonous residues at the first opportunity. But no, they are much too valuable for that. He waits until he is threatened with attack, and then ejects a drop of this witches' brew in the enemy's direction. Exit the aggressor.

Some kinds of sea slug put on an even more brilliant performance.[5] They are very partial to certain members of the Coelenterata family,[6] which most sea creatures avoid because they are covered with stings of the whiplash type. These weapons are normally coiled up, but if a fish comes too close they fly out and sting it.

Somehow the sea slug manages to swallow his prey without getting stung. He seems to know how to put a safety-catch on the whiplash stings, which remain coiled up and therefore harmless. But he makes no attempt to digest them; instead, he sets about making use of them, just as they are. Nature has provided him with some narrow hair-lined tubes linking his stomach to the surface of his body. Slowly and carefully he works the stings out through these channels and arranges them in strategic positions on his back. Whatever the secret safety-catch may have been, he removes it once the sting is safely positioned, and then he is ready to sting his own enemies with all the confidence of a terrorist holding a captured army rifle.

Once again we are confronted with some incredibly complex mechanisms that could not possibly have evolved – unless nature knew what it was setting out to accomplish and made its long-term plans accordingly. The first insect that stopped eating wholesome food and took to munching the gummy pine needles would have come to a (literally) sticky end. The first sea slug to set up in business as a sting-swallower would have had a very short career.

It stands to reason that wizardry like this can hardly have come into existence on its own, either by evolving in small steps or by just popping up, fully formed. Doesn't it look as if Somebody must have made it on purpose?

Daredevil flies that live on spiders

Another stunt-man of the insect world has only recently been discovered by two research workers in the Central American rain forest. In 1977 they published an account of a tiny fly which spends much of its life in the very last place you would think of looking for a small insect – sitting on the back of a large spider.

This fly indulges in such a seemingly perilous form of hitch-hiking because it has a most unusual way of making a living. The spider it lives on is the handsome *Nephila clavipes*, the golden web spider, which has a strange way of dealing with large, tough insects caught in its web. It injects a dose of digestive juice into the body of the trapped insect, and then waits for it to turn into a tender, sticky mess.

At this point the little fly seizes his opportunity. While

the spider is still waiting for his meal to be done to a turn, the fly hops across and lands on one of the still-solid parts of the melting insect. He pokes his mouth into one of the spreading pools of soup, and drinks. It takes him only a few seconds to gorge himself to the full, because his mouth is specially formed for sucking liquids fast. Before the spider is ready to gobble up his own meal, the satisfied fly is stretched out on his host's back once more, enjoying an after-dinner nap.

Like being shot from a gun twice nightly before a large audience, this is a delightfully easy way of making a living – once you have acquired the knack. But while you are learning the trade it must be a very hazardous affair. As the biologists who discovered this enterprising fly have commented: 'The behaviour [of the flies] requires precise identification of the host and extremely accurate landing, with any error likely to be fatal.'[7]

Any error would be fatal, sure enough. If the fly took up residence on the wrong kind of spider he would starve to death waiting for the soup that the other spiders do not manufacture. And he has to land on a hard portion of the fast-melting insect: if he misjudged his landing place the poor fly would really be in the soup, in more ways than one.

How did this species of fly manage to evolve those two extraordinary abilities of host-identification and pinpoint landing, without becoming extinct while it was still a learner? And how did it come about that he simultaneously evolved the ideal mouth for the job, thus making possible his swift getaway?

The research workers who reported on this skilful insect do not answer those questions. They content themselves with the admission that 'the evolution of the relationship [between fly and spider] must have been long and complex.'[8]

This naive statement must be one of the best examples of missing the obvious since the mountaineer met a one-legged man on top of Snowdon, and concluded that 'this disabled man's climb to the summit must have been long and complex.'

Just as the cripple's presence on the summit testifies to the existence of the Snowdon mountain railway, so the behaviour of these spider-riding flies is one more indication of farsightedness in nature. And farsightedness implies the existence of Someone who knows where nature is going.

Why sex?

For hundreds of millions of years nature seems to have got along very nicely without sex. All the most primitive forms of life reproduce themselves by simply splitting in two. Some quite elaborate plants also, such as ferns, are single-sexed: they produce seed asexually. Trees, which do produce their seeds sexually, can still reproduce themselves quite well without sex by throwing up suckers from their roots. Even female frogs can be made to reproduce themselves in the laboratory without the help of a male. Only the higher animals seem to find sex essential.

Why then, did nature bother to introduce sex at all, if it is not really necessary? Indeed, in terms of survival-power sex is a handicap: in a species where every animal is a female, capable of bearing young, twice as many babies will be born as in a species where half the population are mere males. Consequently, a single-sex species is twice as well-fitted to survive as a two-sex species. If 'the survival of the fittest' is what makes the world tick, why are the less-fit, two-sexed species still here?

Astonishingly, evolutionists never seem to have asked themselves that question until a few years ago. (Or perhaps it is not so astonishing, bearing in mind their dismal track-record where embarrassing questions are concerned.) Anyway, now they have at last recognised the problem they seem to be quite perturbed about it.

The point is that sex gives a species a long-term biological advantage. In a one-sex population, mother and daughter and granddaughter and great-granddaughter would resemble each other almost as closely as identical twins. Not only would this make life more boring, it would in the long run produce a less flexible, less adaptable population, poorly fitted to survive in changing conditions.

So, once again, Mother Nature has been wonderfully farsighted. She introduced sex, even though it brought nothing but a serious biological handicap to its first possessors. She evidently foresaw that in the future some compensating advantages would build up, which eventually would outweigh the disadvantages of sex. Once again, nature seems to have known where she was going – or Somebody did.

What do biologists make of all this? Not much, as yet. Two books on the subject were published recently. One[9] was reviewed by one of Britain's foremost evolutionists, Professor Maynard Smith. He called it an '... infuriating book ... infuriating because it fails, narrowly but decisively, to provide the illumination promised.'[10]

The second book[11] was reviewed by the American professor who wrote the first book. He concluded that its author '... does not, however, manage to come up with a very satisfactory explanation ... The explanation he proposes is historical accident ... *perhaps more adequate hypotheses are in order*'[12] (my italics).

'Historical accident', eh? They must really be scraping the bottom of the barrel if that was still the best available explanation as recently as 1975.

As the review remarked, 'perhaps more adequate hypotheses are in order.'

Well, what's wrong with the hypothesis of a Creator?

'Such views are widespread'

In this chapter we have seen that nature shows many signs of what could be called 'directiveness', or, 'purposiveness', or, 'acting with the future in mind'. Philosophers have a special name for this sort of thing: they call it 'teleology', after a Greek word meaning the fulfilment of a purpose.

In the first half of the nineteenth century people saw teleology everywhere in nature. Then Darwin revolution-ised mankind's way of thinking. He convinced most of the world's intellectuals that nothing in biology – not even superbly efficient mechanisms like the human eye – was designed for a purpose, since everything just evolved.

Whether Darwin quite convinced himself is doubtful. In 1860 he wrote to his colleague Asa Gray:

> I remember the time when the thought of the eye made me cold all over, but I have got over this stage of the complaint, and now small trifling particulars of struc-ture often make me very uncomfortable. The sight of a feather in a peacock's tail, whenever I gaze at it, makes me sick![13]

The then Duke of Argyle has left an account of a con-versation when Darwin was on his deathbed. The Duke referred to various wonderful devices of nature, and asked Darwin if he could not see that these must be the work of a Mind. He wrote:

> I shall never forget Darwin's answer. He looked at me very hard and said: 'Well, that often comes over me with overwhelming force, but at other times', and he shook his head vaguely, adding, 'it seems to go away.'[14]

Until recently most of Darwin's admirers had no such doubts. But now a most surprising change has taken place. *Teleology is creeping back into biology.* It seems the evidence for it is so strong that many biologists cannot shut their eyes to it any longer.

Hard-line unbelievers are clearly rattled by the trend.

113

Maynard Smith, for instance, in the review quoted above, wrote:

Panglossianism[15] ... can be defined as the belief that the characteristics of organisms exist to ensure the survival of species and of ecological communities. [In other words, the belief that nature knows where she is going!] Although accusations of Panglossianism are usually indignantly denied, *such views are widespread* among evolutionists, ecologists and ethologists ... It is true that Panglossianism is rife, but it is not universal. *Other evolutionists have been attempting non-teleological explanations* of these phenomena. (My italics)

Only a small minority of European and American biologists believe in the Christian doctrine of creation. There would not be enough of them to make up the large army of Panglossians and teleologists that Maynard Smith is worried about. Evidently there are many biologists who cannot yet bring themselves to accept the creative God of the Bible, but who nevertheless realise there must be some sort of supernatural intelligence in, or behind, this wonderful world of ours.

Considering the strength of the evidence this is not really surprising. To the believer it is a very encouraging and reassuring trend. It is long overdue.

Chapter 8

THE MIRACLE IN THE MIRROR

To see some really convincing evidence that God exists, take a look in a mirror.

Homo sapiens ('Man the Wise One') they call us. There are two alternative explanations of our origin.

The oldest one is that 'God created man in His own image.'[1] The more recent alternative is that man just happened to evolve by a series of lucky chances – and that then man proceeded to create an imaginary god in *his* own image. Which is right?

Beware of thinking that the question has already been settled, just because of what the biology books say. Biologists themselves are the first to warn us not to believe all that we read in the textbooks on this subject.

For example, in 1975 a leading American anthropologist wrote a survey of present knowledge concerning our supposed African ancestors. This is how he began:

An important part of today's conventional wisdom about human evolution is based on studies of teeth, jaws and skull fragments of australopithecine fossils. That these fossils are undoubtedly closely related to the human lineage is now engrained into textbooks ... *Some investigators have long disagreed ... more recently other workers have also begun to question accepted views.*[2] (My italics)

The popular idea that science has the question of our ancestry all buttoned up is on a par with Santa Claus – a nice tale for toddlers. The fact that so many adults believe it merely shows how well some scientists can bluff their way.

115

Fortunately, there are still plenty of honest anthropologists around to make admissions like this: 'As we go farther back in time, there is *less evidence* ... it is only through *speculation* that we may gain some insights into what the life of our ancestors *may* have been'[3] (my italics).

The nature of man's origin is still very much of an open question among scientists. Consequently, we can well afford to follow their example and approach it with an open mind.

Man the misfit

Man has always been an also-ran in the race for survival. Even today, man's continued existence is hanging on a hair. Our race lives trembling for fear that we shall pollute ourselves into extinction, or starve because of the population explosion, or blow the world to bits.

A few thousand years ago the future must have looked equally hazardous for prehistoric man. Of all the creatures of the wild his body must have been about the worst fitted for survival. Yet he has survived. How?

Beware of the glib answer, 'through his brain.' The man who first said that must have been a bit short of the grey stuff himself. All the evidence suggests that brawn and instinct are the best ingredients for a survival kit; high intelligence is a poor substitute for those.

Look at the dinosaurs. Those hulking brutes with their pinhead brains were the masters of the earth for well over a hundred million years. During that time they coped successfully with some catastrophic changes in their environment. Why they died out is still a mystery, but it certainly was not because they were pushed into extinction by the brainier mammals: those only came along millions of years after the dinosaurs had departed.

Beef, not brain, was the formula for success in the dinosaur's day. Away from civilisation it is still much the same today. Who in his senses would pick a flabby-

muscled mathematical genius as a companion for a perilous trek through the jungle, if he could have the choice of
a six-foot bricklayer with nothing to boast about except
common sense and biceps like car tyres?

Brain or no brain, man is largely a misfit in the primeval forest. There must be some reason for his survival,
but whatever it is it isn't merely his brain.

The real secret of our survival

The lion is not really the king of beasts. In order to survive, every animal has to be able to make Leo look silly
in one way or another. Some take to the trees, some to the
water, some disappear down holes. Others just rely on
breeding so fast that he can't eat them all. The elephant
and the crocodile can defeat a lion in a straight fight, and
many animals can leave him standing when it comes to a
race. But almost the only thing poor old *Homo sapiens*
can beat Leo at is a game of chess.

Fortunately, man has another defence against him.
Lions happen to dislike human flesh. Admittedly, there
are such things as man-eating lions. But they are rare
freaks, like Siamese twins. When a maneater does appear
he causes appalling havoc in the African bush – enough
to show that primitive man could never have survived in
lion country if all lions were maneaters.

Apart from crocodiles, which man can easily avoid by
keeping away from the water, the only large African car-
nivore with a partiality for human flesh is the hyena. And
the hyena is the most timid of all the big beasts of prey:
despite their love of human meat hyenas will never attack
a man unless he is wounded or asleep.

Outside Africa the picture is much the same. The only
other large creatures that delight in human flesh are
aquatic, like certain kinds of shark, and man can easily
keep out of their way. The really dangerous flesh-eating
land animals will not touch human beings except as a last
resort.

Man evidently owes his survival to this extraordinary

fact. If the widespread lion, wolf and bear had the same taste in meat as the shark, the crocodile and the cautious hyena, man would long be extinct.

To attribute this to mutation and natural selection is clearly absurd. Man's flesh is not *generally* unpalatable, otherwise hyenas and crocodiles and the occasional man-eating lion and tiger (to say nothing of cannibals) would not find it so attractive. It is *specifically* unpalatable to just those species that would otherwise threaten man's existence.

The odds against such a tailor-made mutation occurring by chance, at just the right point in man's short history, are unimaginably large. In statisticians' jargon, 'Effective probability – zero!'

Once more the evidence points to a familiar conclusion. Something, or Somebody, appears to be looking after man's interests. Nature – or nature's Master – had a purpose in mind, in making things the way they are.

Threat from the insect world

The thought of a world full of man-eating wolves is horrendous enough. But the thought of man-eating insects is even worse.

This is not just fantasy. Even very small insects can be lethal in large numbers. On many occasions a disabled man has been eaten alive by swarms of tropical ants.

Larger insects can sometimes be deadly on their own. That fearsome arachnid, the black widow spider, has killed many a strong man. Fortunately for us, these creatures do not prey on man and only use their lethal weapons in self-defence. Just imagine what life would be like in the tropics if their favourite food happened to be human meat ...

Or think of the clouds of tiny European midges and gnats that come hunting for their modest portions of human blood. They might have happened to have bodies as big as dragonflies, in which case human life in Europe would have been impossible.

There is a freshwater fish in South America called the piranha, with a body no larger than a rat. Yet if a shoal of piranhas come across a man swimming they will reduce him to a skeleton within a few minutes. It is a remarkable piece of good fortune for us that piranhas are fish and not animals. Suppose that rats, for instance, possessed the same shaped jaws and the same appetites as piranhas; who would then be the undisputed masters of the earth, they or us?

No, let us not deceive ourselves. It does indeed look as if man owes his survival to a mind. But not to his own puny mind. It seems much more likely that man is here because the Mind behind nature has kept all our potential executioners in check.

How did man acquire his brains?

We have seen that there are a great many missing rungs in the ladder of life. Evolutionists believe there has been continuous, gradual progress. But the facts of geology and biology do not support this idea. The record is full of gaps, and life appears to have advanced in a series of great leaps across them.

Now we come to the biggest gap of all – the huge gulf separating man's brain from that of the animals.

The cleverest animal, the chimpanzee, is still only on the same level as a bright two-year-old boy or girl. (As the statistician remarked, 'That means a two-year-old chimp has an IQ of 100; aren't chimps wonderful!' – an interesting illustration of how statistics can be used to mislead people.) If man is really only a 'naked ape', how did he acquire a brain that, although only a little bigger, can sometimes be a million times more powerful than that of the apes?

The best that evolutionists can do is to put it down to man's use of tools. The argument runs like this: 'As soon as man began to use tools, the cleverer men were immediately at a big advantage. They survived, while the dullwits died out. Thus natural selection transformed Man the Toolmaker from a shambling near-animal into a superb thinker.'

This sounds plausible until you ponder it. Then you realise that it won't do, for several reasons:

(1) As we have already noted, as a means of surviving in wild country, even high intelligence is a poor substitute for animal instinct coupled with animal muscle. The small differences in intelligence that natural selection is supposed to have worked on would have had even less effect. The toughest toolmakers are those most likely to have survived, rather than the brainiest.

(2) 'Man the toolmaker' is a misleading piece of flattery. 'Man the weapon-maker and skull-basher' might be a more accurate description, both of early man and twentieth-century man. Who knows whether modern man is going to use atomic power to save lives peaceably or to decimate the human race in war? And who knows whether early man's 'tools' saved more lives in time of peace than they destroyed in times of anger?

(3) The only people whose brains unquestionably helped early man to survive were the great inventors. But you can bet a pound to a penny that the men who first tamed fire, developed agriculture, or dreamed up the wheel, did not benefit at all in the Darwinian sense. Probably they and all their immediate relatives were soon murdered out of jealousy by the muscular blockheads from across the river.[4] Even the genius who gave the world the dubious benefit of the bow and arrow could well have been clubbed to death as he sat wondering how he could improve on his invention.

(4) The really big difference between man's brain and the animals' is that man can think on two different levels. Like the animals, man can think about things he experiences: food, and drink, and enemies, and birth, and death. But unlike the animals, man can think on another

120

level. He can think *abstractly* of truth, and probability, and consequence, and illogicality; he can be a mathematician, or a philosopher, or a theoretical physicist, or a concocter of theories of man's origin. And the more high-powered his thinking becomes, the less likely it is to help him survive in the bush. (The jungles of Westminster and Wall Street are another matter, of course.)

Talking and doing

Man's brain on its own would not take him very far. The dolphin has a good brain as animal brains go; for all we know it might be a great deal better than a chimpanzee's. But however good it is, a dolphin cannot exploit his brain to the full. He is unable to achieve much because he has no hands. And he cannot pass on the benefits of his own experience to his children very well, because a string of clicking noises is a poor substitute for speech.

Man's brain and voice are obviously in a class of their own. But don't underestimate his hands, which are far above anything the animal world possesses. Without them man could never get the best out of his brain. Imagine trying to assemble a television set or carry out heart surgery with an octopus's tentacle, an elephant's trunk, or even a monkey's paw!

This is all very difficult for the evolutionist to explain. Why should the one species have evolved, simultaneously, the best brain, the best method of communication, and the best handling gear as well? Doesn't this look much more like the result of design on Somebody's part, than the result of chance mutations?

True, there is an obvious connection between language and intelligence. They might just conceivably have evolved together as a linked pair, as many evolutionists believe, but this is still very far from being proved. The whole area still bristles with difficulties. As an evolutionist recently admitted: 'The origin of human language is clearly one of the two main remaining problems of human evolution.'[5]

The crux of the problem is this. Human language is infinitely more subtle and complex than the simple needs of survival would demand. According to evolutionary theory, you would expect primitive peoples to evolve a primitive language; then, as civilisations became more complex, their languages should become more and more advanced.

In fact, the very opposite seems to have occurred. As one evolutionist, taking pains not to overstate the difficulty, has put it: 'The fact is that many "primitive" languages aren't any more primitive than most of the rest of the culture; indeed, they are often a great deal more complex and more efficient than the languages of the so-called higher civilisations.'[6]

Then there is the problem of the speech organs themselves. These are far more elaborate than we need for communicating. Have you ever heard a man who has had his voice-box removed because of throat cancer and has learnt to speak without it? You can understand every word he says. But something is sadly lacking: he cannot convey emotion by subtle variations in the tone of his voice as we can.

He says, 'I love you!', 'Is that so?', 'One pound thirty,' and, 'I'll kill you!!' all in the same monotone. Yet his meaning is quite clear enough to serve man's basic needs: our wonderful speech apparatus is nothing more than a delightful luxury from a biological point of view.

When we contemplate that incredible combination of a superb brain, superb speech organs, and a superb pair of hands, only one conclusion is possible.

As an engineer would put it, these attributes of man are hopelessly 'over-designed' for the simple needs of survival in the wilds. They are much too good for the job, like a Rolls-Royce being used to cart manure around a farm. Yet in nearly every other respect we are badly 'under-designed' for survival.

122

Evolution may seem plausible when it is used to explain how animals developed what they needed for survival. But as an explanation of the body and mind of man it is hopelessly inadequate.

The evidence all seems to point in one direction. As creatures of the wild we are misfits: we don't really belong there. We are very much better suited to a civilised environment – not necessarily the environment provided by our present decadent, mismanaged civilisation, but human society as it could be if only we were to manage our affairs more wisely.

Doesn't it seem likely that Somebody must have designed and created us with this higher destiny in mind?

Doubting Wallace

Many evolutionists have admitted to being very uncomfortable about the facts discussed above. Among them was the famous Alfred Russell Wallace, who collaborated with Darwin in the very first publication on natural selection.

According to the American anthropologist Loren Eiseley, Wallace expressed his doubts in 1869, ten years after Darwin published his *Origin of Species*. Wallace would have appreciated the arguments of this chapter, since he argued that man's brain is far too good to have been produced by natural selection.[7] He wrote:

An instrument has been developed in advance of the needs of its possessor ... Natural Selection could only have endowed the savage with a brain a little superior to that of the ape, whereas he actually possesses one very little inferior to that of the average member of our learned societies.

Darwin was well aware of the seriousness of the objection. He wrote to Wallace: 'I hope you have not murdered too completely your own and my child.'

Built for civilised living

There is also the fact that *Homo sapiens* takes far longer to grow up than any other animal – about a quarter of a normal lifetime. Most mammals our size can take care of themselves when they are a few months old, and are fully grown at two years.

A long childhood is essential if you want your young-sters to get a knowledge of French and history and algebra and domestic science. If all you want is that they should survive in the wilderness, then the sooner they grow up the better. Man's exceptionally long period of adolescence is one more pointer to the fact that we are designed for some far greater purpose than mere survival.

Our lengthy childhood seems to be related to another strange way in which our race is unique: we are the only creatures that have a menopause.[8] Many a worn-out wife, in the days before family planning became wide-spread, has thanked God for this blessing. Were they right in regarding their menopause as a gift from God? Or is there any reason to think we evolved it?

All the evidence points in the same direction. There appears to be no way in which a menopause makes a race of animals fitter to survive. What it does is to make life sweeter, both for mothers and their children.

Since every boy and girl needs a Mum until they are grown up, it is a very good thing for them that every woman becomes infertile about twenty years before her threescore years and ten is up. Civilised family life would suffer enormously if this were not so.

But ask any primitive tribesman if he wishes his wife could go on bearing children all her life. He would reply, 'Of course. It would benefit the tribe. If she dies while some children are young, other women will gladly bring them up. The more children we have, the more chance there is that a fair number will survive.' If he were a very intelligent tribesman he might add, 'After all, that's how it is in the animal world. Why not with us?'

Indeed, why not, if man is only a highly-evolved animal?

It goes without saying that evolutionists have answers to these questions. They are bound to. With a certain type of evolutionist, rule number one is, 'Never admit you're stumped. Produce a solution to every difficulty, even if it means making a wild guess. Even an absurdly improbable explanation is better than nothing.'

The length to which evolutionists will go rather than admit defeat is almost unbelievable. For example, Richard Dawkins recently had another shot at explaining the menopause.[9] Children born of old women, he argues, would be weaklings. It is better that they should be 'sacrificed' (by not being born) for the sake of the children born to younger women. This will benefit those other children, and hence the race, in the long run.

But if Mum must stop being a mother when she is fifty so as to be a good granny, what about Dad. Why doesn't he have a menopause, too? Easy, says Dawkins. Dad can marry another wife, a young one, when he is old, and it might benefit the race for him to have children by her. The fact that it would obviously benefit the race more for that woman to marry a younger man does not seem to occur to him!

And what about the animals? The same arguments can be applied to them, to 'prove' that they, too, would benefit from having a menopause. Why, then, does none of the animals have one? Dawkins cannot answer that, and neither can any other evolutionist, although many have tried.

An ape with the soul of a poet?

If man is really only a super-beast, how does he come to have the soul of a poet? Man can contemplate the majesty of the universe, the affection of a woman for her child, or the horror of death – he can dwell on these things and a myriad other aspects of the mystery of life, until they fill him with awe. A few gifted individuals can express these feelings in sublime words, words which will stir the hearts of millions in years to come.

Where is the survival value of all that? If man's poetic soul evolved, why did it evolve, and how?

Our very senses are designed to serve the artist within us, rather than our need for survival. Why did not primitive man evolve the eyes of a hawk, which would have been so much more useful than our own in the wild?

As it is, we have eyes that are exquisitely built for a very different end. They can detect the subtlest variations in light and shade, in tone and tint and hue and depth of colour. With eyes like ours we can fully appreciate the glory of a sunset, or the ravishing beauty of a great work of art. No animal's eye would serve us half as well for this purpose.

So with our hearing also. Most creatures of the wild can detect, amidst all the other sounds of the forest, the rustle of a leaf disturbed by a stalking predator's paw. Not so with our race: the slinking cobra can approach within striking distance before man hears a sound.

Our ears, like so much of us, were obviously made for a higher purpose. Inadequate in the forest, they are ideal for the concert hall. With them we can delight in the song of a bird, the ripple of a child's laughter, and all the other soul-stirring tones that our race's amazing larynx can produce.

Again, there is smell. A buffalo can scent a lion a quarter of a mile away, where a man would not notice it until it sprang. Many animals can detect the smell of a distant watercourse, but man could die of thirst three feet from a hidden well. As a tool for survival our nose rates two out of ten.

Yet life for civilised man is greatly enriched by his impractical sense of smell. Who would want to change noses with a buffalo, at the cost of never again delighting in the fragrance of a rose, the aroma of roasting coffee, and the scent of new-mown hay?

Drawing and joking

The psychologist Dr John Kennedy has made a study of man's ability to draw pictures. After years of research, he expressed his conclusions in a scientific paper with the title, 'Drawing was discovered, not invented.'[10]

A colleague of his spent a year with a primitive tribe in Papua, the Songe, who never draw. Yet when they were shown drawings for the first time they did not need to be taught to understand them: they knew, intuitively, what a drawing is.

Kennedy has also made drawings of raised lines and given them to people who were born blind, so that they could feel them. He says: 'I expected these would be meaningful only after training ... We have been surprised. Some congenitally blind subjects can identify as many simple line drawings as blindfolded sighted people, even though they have never had outline drawings before.'

These are only two examples of the wealth of evidence produced by Kennedy, showing that the ability to grasp what a line-drawing stands for is born in us.

Another strange power that baffles psychologists is man's ability to see the funny side of life. A few unfortunate people are born without a sense of humour, but most of us possess it in greater or lesser degree.

Different races develop their senses of humour along different lines, just as they have developed different forms of music. So have people in different periods of history. But the basic ability to joke and to laugh is a deep-seated property of the human mind. It makes civilised life sweeter, both in good days and in times of adversity. As a part of our cultural make-up it is indispensable. But it is hardly likely to have helped the cave-men to survive.

In Wallace's revealing phrase, all these abilities of the human mind – the appreciation of logic, of beauty, of poetry, of music, of delightful smells, of drawing, and of jokes – were 'developed in advance of the needs of their possessor'. To account for them as the product of natural

127

forces alone is impossible. Somebody once asked Einstein if he thought that we might, one day, be able to explain everything in scientific terms. He replied: 'Yes that is conceivable, but *it would make no sense*. It would be as if one were to reproduce Beethoven's Ninth Symphony in the form of an air pressure curve'[11] (my italics).

Einstein was right. It makes no sense to explain the Ninth Symphony as merely a particular pattern of air pressure pulsations. And it similarly makes no sense to explain Beethoven himself as merely the result of random forces and natural selection.

Man the musician, man the creative artist, man the dreamer, man the inventor, man the thinker – this extraordinary creature simply cannot have evolved just through the need to survive. He must surely have been created for a purpose, to be something more than the lord of the animal kingdom.

Man's profoundest art

A hundred years ago a Scottish journalist, Robert Roberts, used the existence of sex as an argument for the existence of God. It was a courageous thing to do in the religious climate of Victorian Britain, and Roberts was clearly diffident about it. 'Don't wince,' he admonished his readers, 'I am dealing simply with a fact.'[12]

Although the climate of opinion is much less frigid today, I can still share the nineteenth-century writer's feelings of self-consciousness. Yet the argument is so powerful that it cannot be left unspoken. As Roberts put it, please don't wince: I am only going to deal with a fact.

In the animals, sex meets one need and only one: the reproduction of the species. Accept if you will that it was created, or argue if you like that it was evolved. All of us are agreed on this: the purpose of the sex instinct in the animals is simply reproduction, and it serves that purpose well.

With man the situation is very different. The contrast

128

can be pointed out like this: *animals mate, but human beings make love.*

If man is only an animal writ large, why this difference? Mating would ensure the survival of our species just as well as making love.

As it is, lovemaking by a married couple is the profoundest art form known to the poetic soul of man. Here, at least four of the five senses – sight, sound, touch, and smell – can play their part. And even this is only a beginning: on that physical foundation can be erected a union of two beings where the mental, the emotional and the spiritual are subtly and exquisitely intertwined.

Sadly, it is possible for every art form to be debased (and in our age, it seems, most of them are). Marital love in our sick civilisation is constantly being perverted, corrupted, commercialised, dehumanised and dragged down almost to the purely physical level of the animals. And marriages – even Christian marriages – can all too easily fall far short of the ideal.

But all this makes no difference to the basic facts. The heights are still there, ready to be scaled, or at least approached, by every loving man and wife that will. And they still present a riddle that evolution cannot solve.

Why is a woman so made that the physical act brings little pleasure to her unless she feels needed, cared for, loved? Why do both husband and wife only find their deepest joy when each seeks first and foremost to fulfil the needs of the other – a principle taught by the apostle Paul in a sadly neglected passage: 'For the wife does not rule over her own body but the husband does; likewise the husband does not rule over his own body, but the wife does.'[13]

How can we explain all these wonders of our own mind and body?

Were blind chance and vibrating atoms really the father and mother of a thousand miracles?

Or did a wise and loving Creator make us so?

Beyond the five senses

There remains one last reason for believing that man's mind is far more marvellous than many scientists will admit.

For an obvious reason, atheistic scientists have often ridiculed the idea of telepathy. If human minds can communicate telepathically, it means there is something in this universe that science cannot detect or understand. And that could prove to be the thin end of a very big wedge: it might turn out to be the first step towards recognising the existence of spirit beings – and God.

Despite their prejudices, however, many scientists have become persuaded lately that some men and women really do possess a sixth sense. More and more experiments in this field are being carried out, and some remarkable results have been obtained. There is space here to mention only one.

In 1974 Uri Geller's telepathic claims were investigated by a group of scientists at the Stanford Research Institute in California. Their report[14] caused a considerable stir in scientific circles.

Most of these experiments with Geller were of a very complex nature and yielded inconclusive results. Scientists are still arguing about them. But one was so simple that no argument seems possible.

A dice was put in a locked steel box which was shaken and placed on a table. Geller was asked if he could tell the number on the dice. His written prediction (if any) was noted by the experimenters present, who then unlocked the box to see what the dice really said.

The experiment was repeated ten times. Twice Geller said he could not tell. The other eight times he claimed that he could, and wrote down his prediction of the number. And eight times out of eight he was correct.

The odds against achieving this by guessing are more than a million to one. There appears to be no way in which Geller could have cheated. And it seems hardly likely that two serious research workers in a reputable laboratory would enter into a conspiracy with Geller to deceive the public.

The only other alternative is to conclude that there really is such a thing as 'second sight', and that Geller, on some occasions at least, possesses it. Once more we are faced with an indication that the human mind is a wonderful device – much too wonderful to have evolved on its own.

We are not done yet with the evidence that man was made in his Creator's image. The most powerful argument of all has been reserved for the next chapter but one.

But first we must make a digression, to look at a problem which troubles many would-be believers.

Chapter 9

INTERLUDE – IS GOD UNFAIR?

He was a scruffy little fellow, the kind that normally would not be worth a second glance. Several times he had tried to distract my audience at Speakers' Corner, in London's Hyde Park, but no one took much notice of him.

Then he played his ace of trumps.

'I don't believe in this God of yours,' he shouted. 'If He really exists, why doesn't He show Himself? I challenge Him: if there really is a God, let Him strike me down dead – now!'

There was an icy silence as all eyes were fixed on the brash character. For a long, tense moment everybody waited to see what would happen. Nothing did. Then the man himself broke the spell.

'See what I mean? Why didn't He do it, if He exists?'

Cackling in triumph he strutted off, and I tried to resume my meeting. But he had achieved his object. My audience was not the same after the interruption. That was my own fault – I was not quick witted enough to reply:

'Don't worry, friend, He will, if you go through life like that. But He will decide the time and the place and the manner of your death Himself. Why should He let you dictate terms to Him?'

'Why doesn't God . . .'

People are always asking why God does not do this, that or the other. I have even seen a printed poster on a wall asking why God does not stop the 'Troubles' in Northern Ireland.

It is not only unbelievers. Believers also are often

heard to ask why God acts (or fails to act) in the way that He does. Questions of this kind were asked by some of the holiest of men, whose words are preserved for us in the pages of the Bible.[1]

Such questions are perfectly reasonable, so long as they are genuine appeals for an answer and not merely excuses to rebel against religion. They stem from the feeling that if God is perfect, then He ought to be fair and reasonable in all His dealings with mankind. Yet sometimes He seems to be downright unfair and unreasonable. Why is this?

Before we start looking for an answer to this question we must remember one vital fact. In the nature of things, we are not likely to find an explanation that satisfies us completely. Since God is infinite, we are hardly likely to be able to understand His methods perfectly.

In many ways we are like a young child who has been told that he cannot go out to play with his friends, but must stay indoors by himself. To him this seems all wrong. He knows he has been a good boy, and yet he is being punished. His mother is being most unfair – or so it seems to him.

Meanwhile, the mother has tried to explain to the youngster that there is an epidemic of gastro-enteritis in the neighbourhood and she wants to shield him from it. The child in unimpressed. At his age he is incapable of appreciating facts like that. Even the simple statement, 'Mummy loves you, and Mummy knows best', leaves him cold. So he throws a tantrum.

We must take care to avoid behaving like three-year-olds. When Bible characters like Job asked why God was treating them (as they saw it) unfairly, the reply amounted to, 'God loves you, and God knows best.'

We can actually go quite a bit further than that in our search for explanations of God's way of working. But we must not expect to be able to understand every last detail. Our minds are too puny for that.

The problem of doubt

The man in Hyde Park was raising what one might call the 'problem of doubt'. If God wants people to believe in Him, why doesn't He make it obvious that He exists? Why does He leave so much room for doubt?

This is one of the easiest of the 'Why-doesn't-God' questions. Suppose for a moment that God made His presence felt all the time – that every action of ours, good or bad, brought an immediate response from Him in the form of reward or punishment. What sort of a world would this be then?

It would resemble, on a grander scale, the dining room of a hotel in Africa where I once stayed for a few days. The European owner evidently did not trust his African waiters. He would sit on a raised platform at one end of the room, constantly watching every movement. Goods that might possibly be pilfered, such as tea bags, sugar knobs and even pats of butter or margarine, were doled out by him in quantities just sufficient for the needs of the moment. He would scrutinise every bill like Sherlock Holmes looking for signs of foul play.

The results of all this supervision were painfully obvious. I have stayed in many hotels around the world, including a dozen or so in five African countries, but never have I met such an unpleasant bunch of waiters as in that hotel. Their master's total lack of trust in them had warped their personalities. As long as he was watching they acted discreetly, but the moment they thought his guard was down they would seize the opportunity to misbehave.

In much the same way, it would ruin our own characters if God's presence were as obvious as that of the great white chief in his African restaurant. This would then be a world without trust, without faith, without unselfishness, without love – a world where everybody obeyed God because it paid them to do so. Horrors!

So God deliberately maintains a low profile, knowing

that this will bring out the best from at least some part of mankind.

The problem of evil

A much more difficult question is: 'Why doesn't God make this world a better place? Is it because He *can't*? (Because, if so, He cannot be an almighty God.) Or is it because He *won't*? (In which case, He must be lacking in love.)'

This is what philosophers call the 'problem of evil'. Unbelieving philosophers regard it as the only positive reason for believing that God cannot exist.[2] We must therefore examine it very closely.

The first thing to notice is this. The question, 'Why doesn't God make this world a better place?' assumes something. It takes it for granted that the world is not what it ought to be, and that, given a free hand and the necessary power, any Tom, Dick or Harry could soon put it right.

This is not necessarily true. The world is a very, very complex system, and there is a well-known trap for people who want to improve it. When you make a change for the better in one area, you frequently find that you have made things worse in some other way.

An obvious example is the way some drugs have serious side-effects. I once visited a friend in hospital who was being treated for arthritis. He was a heartbreaking sight.

'They injected me with a powerful new drug,' he explained, ruefully. 'It hasn't done much for my arthritis, and it has sent me blind. A "wonder drug" they called it.

'I'm still wondering!' he added, with a brave attempt at humour.

A better example from the medical field is the question of euthanasia, or mercy-killing. Why aren't people who are dying in agony with terminal cancer allowed to finish life quickly with an injection of poison? Wouldn't the world be a better place if they were? We put our beloved pets to sleep rather than see them suffer. Why not human beings?

There is a simple reason. The great majority of doctors – not just religious doctors, but unbelieving doctors, too – are strongly opposed to it. They believe that if mercy-killing were legalised, doctors and nurses would gradually grow more callous and brutal.

Also, the practice would lead to all sorts of abuses. To cite just one: people looking after invalid relatives could easily murder them by applying psychological pressure if they wanted to be rid of them; they would only need to make an unwanted invalid's life a misery, until eventually the poor wretch took the easy way out and asked for a death-shot.

For these and other reasons, most doctors are convinced that a world where mercy-killing was permitted would be nastier than the world we have now.

Nonsense is always nonsense

One of the most fundamental facts about life is that we cannot eat our cake and have it. It would be very nice if we could, but we can't.

There is a sense in which this is also true about God. It stands to reason that even God, all-powerful though He is, is unable to do a thing and *not* do it at the same time.

This can help us to see a reason for some things which many of us regard as bad. Pain is one of them. If we accidentally pick up a hot iron it hurts, and we drop it before it has time to do any serious damage. Without the pain to warn us we might have held on to the iron until we smelt our flesh burning.

Unbelievers sometimes argue that a kind-hearted God could have given us some other kind of danger signal, something that would not have hurt us, like a bell ringing in the brain. But how do we know that the sound of such a 'bell' would not have distressed us just as much as pain

136

does? And if the 'bell' was deliberately made so that it did not upset us, would we take enough notice of its warnings?

When everything is taken into account it is evident that pain – or something equally unpleasant – is the only kind of danger signal that would work. Without pain the world would be a worse place, on balance, not a better one. Doctors are agreed on that. And even the almighty God cannot both *give* pain and *not give* pain to the world – to say that He could is just meaningless nonsense. As Lewis once said in this connection, 'nonsense remains nonsense even when we talk it about God.'[3]

Adventure is another case in point. Every year many thousands of people spend part of their spare time practising some dangerous sport, for the sake of the thrills it gives them. And every year hundreds of them are drowned, or are smashed into lifeless wreckage when they fall off precipices or their parachutes fail to open or their motorcycles crash.

Wouldn't it be a better world if God provided a sort of miraculous safety net for all these people, to save their lives when things went wrong? Would it?

Ask any rock climber if he would still go climbing if God were to take all the risk out of the sport. Not he! There would be no fun in it if that happened. With no risk, no danger, no excitement and no thrills on the mountains, there wouldn't be any mountaineers either.

Consequently, anyone who thinks that God could improve the world by taking the unhappiness out of it has probably never thought the matter out.

Human happiness is a strange thing. Two of the most obviously happy people I have ever seen were a boy and a girl in London, terribly in love – and both totally blind. Others have been peasant farmers in Africa, with a cash income of less than a pound a week. Some of the most unhappy have included a millionaire businessman, and a group of militant trade unionists eaten up with envy and frustration because this year's massive pay rise was not quite as big as last year's.

With human beings the way they are, who can say for certain what changes would make the world a better place?

Testimony of an unbeliever

The novelist Aldous Huxley must have thought deeply about this subject. In his *Brave New World* he portrayed an England of some future age where science had provided every conceivable ingredient of happiness. Discomfort, pain and suffering had been totally abolished. Everybody was delighted, since they had all brainwashed one another into thinking they were really happy.

Everybody, that is, except for one original thinker, Huxley's hero. People called him the Savage, partly because of his foreign origin and partly because of his rebellious attitude to society. Huxley portrayed him as the only sensible man left alive. This is what the Savage demanded:

'I don't want comfort . . . I want real danger, I want freedom, I want goodness, I want sin.'

'In fact,' said Mustapha Mond, 'you're claiming the right to be unhappy.'

'All right, then,' said the Savage, 'I claim the right to be unhappy.'

And this message does not come from a Christian novelist but from an unbeliever.

The suffering of animals

It is sometimes suggested that at least God might have made a world where animals do not suffer. Surely, it is argued, what Tennyson called 'Nature, red in tooth and claw' is a disgrace; could not God have been kinder to dumb animals?

138

There are two answers to this. First of all, we must not exaggerate the problem by supposing that wild animals have minds like ours. We have a horror of being eaten by wild beasts, but animals clearly do not. Many observers of wild life have testified that animals are quite unconcerned about predators, except at the actual moment of pursuit.[4]

We might wonder how those two rabbits, playing so happily in the sunshine, could be so carefree when there are foxes in the next field. Simple: it is because they are rabbits, and not human beings dressed up as rabbits. Make no mistake, rabbits do not feel about foxes as we feel about lions.

Instead, they probably feel more as we do about road accidents. We know that several hundred thousand people will be killed on the world's roads next year. But we don't tremble with fear every time we step outside the house. We do not recite, 'Road transport, red in tyre and windscreen,' whenever we back the car out of the garage. Nor do we go through life terrified by the thought of all the deadly bacteria and viruses around us.

We simply accept that danger exists, and then forget about it unless and until it strikes. So far as naturalists can tell us that also seems to be how animals regard their natural enemies.

The other thing to remember is that carnivorous animals can actually be a blessing in disguise to the creatures they eat. Strange though this may sound, biologists are convinced that it is so. The following quotation is all the more telling because it comes from the pen of a well-known atheist whose views on science are widely acclaimed:

A species may even depend for its well-being on another species that preys upon it. *Rabbits are better off because stoats exist*, for instance.

In some areas the stoats were killed off by game-keepers because they preyed also on game birds. The

139

rabbits, freed of the menace, multiplied and outran their food supply. Many of them starved, and in the end there were fewer and weaker rabbits than before. Since stoats usually catch and kill the older and weaker rabbits, they serve to keep the rabbits younger and stronger than would be the case otherwise.[5] (My italics)

For similar reasons doctors used to call pneumonia, 'The old man's friend.' Old people suffering a painful, lingering death from some chronic complaint often found a quick release when they caught pneumonia. Nowadays pneumonia can usually be cured, and many sufferers who would gladly die are kept alive to go on suffering.

Who can say for certain whether the world would, on balance, be a better place if stoats and pneumonia germs did not exist?

The problem of human perversity

The more we think about the world's troubles, the more difficult it becomes to say how matters could be improved. Only one thing is absolutely certain: human perversity is the main reason for the mess the world is in.

Some people still blame God for the harm that man does. They say, 'Why doesn't God keep man under control?' or, 'Why didn't God make man a nicer creature than he is?' – or even, 'There can't be a God, or He would never have let man bring the world to its present sorry state!'

This is not a very reasonable approach, as the following story may help to show.

One day around 1950 I was driving my battered old pre-war jalopy through London when I came up behind a gleaming new Rolls-Royce, which, believe it or not, was stuck at the traffic lights. The uniformed chauffeur stepped out, put his shoulder to the door pillar and rocked the car (presumably to free a jammed starter), then returned to his seat and drove off.

Spectators at an event like that are not likely to say, 'That can't possibly have been made by Rolls-Royce – their cars never break down. It must be a Forxhall, being passed off as a Rolls.'

They are much more likely to remark, 'Look at that – there's a Rolls-Royce that's gone wrong!'

Similarly, when we look at the human race, with all its pride and greed and cruelty and wretchedness, there are two possible lines we can take.

We can say, 'This race can't have been made by God – one of His creations would never behave as badly as that. It must be a product of evolution, which religious people are trying to pass off as a creation of God.'

Or we can say, 'Look, there's one of God's creatures gone wrong!' This, in fact, is just what the third chapter of the Bible does say.

The question is: can we accept the Bible's explanation? Is it likely that God would allow one of His creatures to 'go wrong'?

Free will

The answer is as simple as the question. Of course God would allow man to 'go wrong' if He decided to give man free will. There would be no alternative. As we have already seen, even an all-powerful Being cannot both *give* a thing and *not give* it at the same time. To say otherwise is to talk childish nonsense.

It would take a brave man – or a very foolish one – to assert that the world would be a better place if God had not given us free will. When I think of those waiters in the African hotel I shudder at the thought of a world where God controlled our every move.

One thing in particular could not exist without free will: love. Human hatred is a terrible evil, and without free will we could not hate one another. But we should not be able to love one another, either. As it is, we have the freedom to manifest either love or hatred. The choice (thank God!) is ours.

It would be wrong to minimise the horrors of man's inhumanity to man. The torture chamber, the bomb that blows little children to bits, the shooting of innocent hostages – things like this are a disgrace to the whole human race. But they are part of the price we have to pay for the freedom to love – or to hate.

Without them, we should never have known of the love of Jonathan who risked his own life to save his friend David from being murdered; nor of the love of the repentant sinner who washed her Lord's feet with her tears; nor of the love of the Lord Jesus Christ Himself, who laid down His life for His friends.[6]

Without this freedom of choice, men and women today would be nothing more than robots. Generosity, kindness, big-heartedness, forgiveness, unselfishness, spontaneous giving, and all the other things that make life worth living could not exist. Life without free will would be life without love.

And life without love would be a living death.[7]

Superbeast, or near-angel?

Man is an extraordinarily mixed-up creature. We are so used to this that it no longer astonishes us. But it is an astonishing fact, none the less.

Every individual man or woman behaves almost like two personalities in one body. Sometimes they act almost like angels, and we say, 'Oh, isn't he a dear!' Then they do something to spoil it, and we complain, 'He got out of bed on the wrong side today!' And, of course, 'he' has exactly the same two views of us, in our own changing moods.

Even though some people may appear to behave well all the time, while others appear to be consistently beastly, the strange mixture still appears in their personalities. The worst type of criminal is still capable of an occasional act of superb unselfishness. And the saintliest of men can sometimes catch themselves acting despicably, as the writers of the Bible frequently admit.[8]

How are we going to explain this strangely mixed character of man? There are two possibilities.

The evolutionist's explanation is that man is a super-beast, an animal on his way up the ladder. He has not yet grown out of all his beastliness, but give him time, and he will gradually reach perfection.

But this starry-eyed view simply does not fit the facts. There is no evidence that modern man is any better *at heart* than his savage ancestors in the Stone Age. As soon as the restraints of civilisation are cast off – as they were by many Nazis in World War II – man shows himself in his true colours. Man is somewhat of a beast, yes, but decidedly not 'on the way up'.

The explanation of the Bible makes far better sense. It tells us that in the first place God created man in His own image, only a little lower than the angels.[9] But then this near-angel[10] misused his free will and allowed himself to be dragged down, nearer to the level of the beasts. Hence our strangely mixed make-up: we are creatures in the image of God, but that image has become sadly tarnished.

Sometimes people ask why God allowed the world to carry on after man went off the rails. They suggest (with tongue in cheek, usually) that it would have been better if God had wiped out our crooked race in the early days, and made a fresh start with a new race.

That would have been one way out, to be sure. But would it have been the best way? If you have a sick animal, there are two courses you can take. You can put it out of its misery quickly; or you can be patient with it, and lovingly care for it until it is well again.

The Bible tells us that God has chosen to nurse our ailing race back to health. The cure is taking a long time, and at present only a small part of mankind is accepting

143

treatment, but the ultimate end is sure. Every Christmas we are reminded of God's promise that one day there really will be, 'Peace on earth, good will toward men'.

In the light of all we know about man and his history, there can be little doubt that the Bible's explanation is the one that best fits the facts.

Determinism

The unbeliever has only one answer to all this, and a very strange answer it is, too. According to him there is no such thing as free will; we *think* we have it, but this is only an illusion. In reality, says the unbeliever, everything we think or say or do is controlled by the glands and cells and molecules in our body, along with the circumstances surrounding us.

This theory is called 'determinism'. (If it strikes you as obvious nonsense, you can skip this section. But because there are many people who treat determinism seriously I shall have to spend a page or two explaining why it may confidently be rejected.)

The first objection to determinism is this. Scientists and philosophers are stricter nowadays than they used to be about holding theories. In the good old days you could hold any theory you liked – for example, that Julius Caesar's grandmother liked her eggs soft boiled.

Today, anybody seriously holding a theory like that would be regarded as an idiot. Such a theory could never be proved wrong, but it could never be proved right, either. Modern thinkers say – very reasonably – that theories are not worth holding unless there is some conceivable way of testing them.

A good many ancient theories fall foul of this very sensible rule. One is the Moslem theory that the universe keeps disappearing and has to be recreated by God each time. This is said to happen many times a second – so fast, in fact, that we do not notice the gaps in between, and so the universe looks permanent to us.

An ingenious theory. But there is no way we could ever test it. Therefore it makes no sense to hold it.

Another ancient theory, which goes back to the Greeks, is called 'solipsism'. A solipsist is a person who says, 'I know that I exist, because I am consciously thinking. But I don't know whether you exist, or anybody else for that matter. You might all be figments of my imagination!'

Once again, it is an ingenious theory, but incapable of proof or disproof. So it is best forgotten.

Determinism is a third ancient theory that is out of place in the modern world. It could not be proved or disproved by any sort of experiment we can imagine, and consequently it should be quietly dropped. Most certainly it should not be used in an argument, because as an unprovable speculation it carries no weight at all.

Very few physical scientists are determinists nowadays. Determinism had its heyday in the late nineteenth century, when physicists believed that the behaviour of dead matter was entirely predictable. So, they argued, perhaps the behaviour of a human mind would be predictable, too, if only one knew enough about the matter it was composed of.

But modern physics has found that the behaviour of most kinds of matter is not so predictable after all. You can predict what a large number of atoms of a substance will do, on average, just as a life assurance company can predict, fairly accurately, how many Englishmen will die next year. But nobody can tell what any individual atom of a liquid or a gas or an unstable solid will do, just as nobody can say for certain when any particular Englishman will die. So it now looks improbable, by analogy with modern physics, that the behaviour of an individual human mind could ever be predicted, or 'determined'.[11]

Determinism, therefore, is both unprovable and unlikely.

But there is an even more serious objection to it. For

the moment, let us suppose that the theory of determinism were true. In that case, whenever we were to think or argue about something, we would not really have any control over our thoughts – they would all be 'determined' in advance. Consequently, the conclusions we came to would not necessarily be correct; whether right or wrong, they would just happen to be the conclusions we were forced to come to!

Even some atheists recognise that this is so. J. B. S. Haldane, for instance, once wrote: 'If my mental processes are determined solely by the motions of atoms in my brain, I have no reason to suppose that my beliefs are true.'[12] Thus, if determinism did happen to be true, we could not possibly *know* that it was true. (Nor could we know anything else to be true, either.)

Determinism must therefore be put firmly where it belongs: in the museum of curious, outdated, illogical, useless speculations.

One final point. Six centuries ago the English philosopher William of Occam laid down a basic principle of sound thinking: never adopt a complicated theory if a simple one will do.

For several good reasons, then, we are bound to conclude that what looks like free will really is free will.

The problem of the black sheep

Atheist writers continually ask why God does not make His professed followers behave a bit better. Charles Gorham, for instance, demands: 'If God started the Reformation, why did he allow many of its leaders to remain narrow-minded, short-sighted and bigoted men? Why did divine influence come so late that Europe had been for more than a thousand years a hot-bed of ignorance, superstition, and variegated morals?'[13] This is a pathetic argument. You might just as well ask, 'If banks are supposed to be a benefit to mankind, why is it that the history of banking is one long story of greed, embezzlement and stick-ups?'

Believers do not claim that religion will automatically improve the characters of all who profess it. Christianity is like education, or marriage: you have to work at it if you want to benefit from it. There will always be lots of university drop-outs, broken marriages, and Judas-like disciples. Well, so what?

We assess the value of education and marriage by their successes, not their failures. Let's be reasonable, and apply the same test to Christianity.

It is curious how unbelievers, in their attempts to charge God with unfairness, are so often unfair themselves. Some of the questions of the 'Why-doesn't-God' type can be answered very easily. Others are more difficult, and can only be answered in a broad, general way.

But at least it is clear that the unbelievers' objections carry little weight. The evidence does not in any way indicate that God is behaving unfairly.

On the contrary, it suggests that He is dealing with an extraordinarily difficult problem (to wit, us!) in a very profound manner.

Chapter 10

INSIDE INFORMATION

I have just spent a whole chapter trying to answer the question, 'Is God unfair?' You may have found the answer convincing, half-convincing, or totally unconvincing, since it is bound to strike different people in different ways. But whatever you think of the answer you are unlikely to regard the question itself as unreasonable.

Though I have heard it discussed many times, I have never yet met anyone who said, 'What does it matter, anyway? Why shouldn't God be unfair if He wants to? Fairness isn't important.'

On the contrary, people are generally very touchy about fairness. Practically everybody agrees that there is such a thing as fair play, and that it matters a lot; that people always ought to deal fairly with each other; and that, if there is a God, He ought to be fair to us.

Now this is really very peculiar. To begin with, it illustrates another vital way in which we differ from the animals. It was noted in chapter 8 that an animal cannot listen to someone arguing a case and say, 'Yes, that's reasonable.' Now we must consider the fact that a real animal is also incapable of saying, like Piggy in the nursery rhyme, 'That's not fair!'

This is not just a question of the animals' inability to talk. The very *ideas* of logic and of fairness apparently do not exist in an animal's mind.

Man's power to think logically is wonderful enough. But our sense of right and wrong is more remarkable still. It throws a lot of light on the question we looked at in the previous chapter: is man a super-beast on the way up, or a near-angel who has fallen down?

Atheists in a tangle

In trying to explain our sense of right and wrong atheists land themselves in a whole web of contradictions.

They usually begin by maintaining that there are really no such things as 'right' and 'wrong'. Slavery, they point out, was regarded as right in first-century Rome and eighteenth-century Europe (and still is in a few countries today) but is outlawed by the whole Western world in our own age. So, they conclude, 'right' merely means, 'what society happens to accept', and 'wrong' means, 'what society decides to condemn'.

This interpretation will not hold water, for several reasons. First of all, it is utterly false to imply that ideas of right and wrong have fluctuated as wildly as fashions in women's clothing. Opinions have varied, and still do vary, on some of the secondary matters. But on the really big issues – like honesty, and truthfulness, and fairness, and courage, and unselfishness – practically all men in practically all ages have been in agreement.

C. S. Lewis was a scholar of world renown, and he provided evidence that the basic moral teaching accepted by the ancient Egyptians, Babylonians, Hindus, Chinese, Greeks and Romans was in every case remarkably similar to that in Europe today.[1] In our own age, the moral standards nominally accepted by the supposedly Christian West, the atheistic Marxist East, and the third world with all its Moslems, Hindus and Buddhists, differ only in relatively small details.

Secondly, where two civilisations differ on some moral principle, each will argue in defence of its own views. Take slavery again, for instance. To be consistent, the atheists should say, 'Slavery is neither right nor wrong in any absolute sense – it merely happens to be something of which our society disapproves.'

But they don't talk like that. Many unbelievers seethe (quite rightly) with moral indignation about the few countries where slavery is still tolerated; they assert that slavery is 'an offence against human rights', and demand that it be abolished everywhere.

When an atheist becomes involved in an argument like that he is really appealing to some higher standard of moral judgement. He is saying, in effect, 'You regard X as right, but I regard Y as right – and my idea of right is *really* right, while you are mistaken.'

So we are back at our starting point. In practice, the unbeliever is convinced that certain things are *really* right. There is room for argument as to what 'really right' consists of. *But that there is such a thing as 'really right' is accepted by everyone when it comes to the crunch.*

Thirdly, most unbelievers are every bit as hypocritical as most Christians in wanting to appear better than they really are. For example, it appears that the majority of the world's police forces use some form of torture to obtain information from people who may or may not be innocent.[2] Yet not one country will openly admit to this. They either say, 'Well, we did once, but now we have stopped,' or, 'If any of our policemen did, he was breaking the rules and will be punished,' or simply, 'It's a lie!'

No country is ever prepared to brazen it out, and say openly, 'Yes, of course we are prepared to risk torturing the innocent sometimes. It is necessary.' Why is this?

Presumably because everybody, believer and unbeliever alike, is well aware that torturing the innocent is an offence against some absolute code of right and wrong. And it is very hard to see how there could possibly be any such absolute standard of right and wrong unless some supreme Lawgiver has provided it.

Could it have evolved?

Ask a well-informed unbeliever where man's sense of right and wrong came from, and he will answer something like this.

'We evolved it, of course, as something that benefits

our race. Man is a social animal, and he could not survive without a set of rules to keep his society running smoothly. You see many signs of unselfish conduct in other social animals, all the way from herds of elephants to hives of bees.'

This reference to animal unselfishness (or 'altruism' as biologists usually term it) is very misleading. It is rather like speaking of hailstones dancing on the pavement; they may *look* as if they are dancing, but that is as far as the resemblance to human dancing goes.

Similarly, animal 'unselfishness' may look like human unselfishness, but is really nothing like it. Human unselfishness is the result of making a choice – often a very difficult choice. But animal 'unselfishness' is an instinct. Animals have very little choice in the matter. To a very large extent, their behaviour is programmed into them.

For example, when a worker bee stings somebody it dies. Its sting is barbed and remains embedded in its victim, with half the bee's body hanging on to it. This does not prevent them from defending their hive and their queen. They will lay down their lives for her at a moment's notice. But there is nothing virtuous about this sort of 'unselfishness'. The bees' behaviour is almost as automatic as a heartbeat.

Now compare this with a case of human unselfishness. Suppose that Buckingham Palace was invaded by terrorists, and a situation arose where the police on duty could only save their queen by sacrificing their own lives. There would be nothing automatic about their behaviour: each man would have to make an agonising moral decision for himself.

This is because there are many instincts in human beings, of which the instinct of self-preservation is one and the instinct to protect women and children is another. But self-preservation is a strong instinct which would urge each man, very powerfully, 'Save yourself – run away,' whereas the much weaker instinct to protect others would only whisper, 'Go on – sacrifice yourself and save your queen.'

In animals, when two instincts are in competition the stronger instinct wins every time. But men are different. In each of us there is a third force at work, a sense of right and wrong, or as those officers in Buckingham Palace would probably call it, a sense of duty. This sits in judgement, so to speak, over the two conflicting instincts and tells us which one we ought to obey.

There is nothing instinctive about this sense of right and wrong. Instincts are neither good nor bad in themselves: what matters is the way we use them. For instance, it is altogether right to let the instinct of self-preservation make us run out of a burning house; but it is wrong to let it make us run out so fast that we leave behind a baby in a cot. Our sense of right and wrong tells us when we ought to obey our instinct of self-preservation, and when we ought to keep it under control.

You can liken the sense of right and wrong to an instructor giving us our first driving lesson. From time to time he says, 'Now accelerate – now brake gently – now change to top gear – now turn left.'

Just as some driving instructors are much better trained than others, our sense of right and wrong also needs training before it can become a reliable guide. People with mistaken ideas of right and wrong have either been to the wrong training school, or have not paid sufficient attention to their lessons.[3]

But the point is that we are all born with the potential to develop such a guide. How did man come by this remarkable sense of right and wrong? It is nothing like an instinct; it is as different from our instincts – and as far above them – as a driving instructor is from the controls of a car.

To say that it might have evolved out of our animal instincts is like imagining that perhaps stones could turn themselves into loaves of bread.

Rebels all

The strangest thing about this sense of right and wrong is that we so often go against it. When I was a young man an older friend advised me, 'Whenever you are in doubt as to what is the right thing to do, decide which course you would prefer to take, and then do the opposite!'

This was a deliberate overstatement, of course. But there is a lot of truth in it. Far more often than not, when we stand at a crossroads in life, our sense of right and wrong tells us that we ought to take the more difficult road. And more often than we like to admit we ignore its advice and take the easy, selfish way.

Nothing quite like this ever happens in the animal world. So far as we can tell, an animal simply obeys whichever instinct happens to be pulling most strongly at the time, then thinks no more about it. With a dog, for instance, loyalty and obedience to its pack-leader is one of the strongest instincts – hence the wonderful, almost flawless, devotion of dogs to their acknowledged masters.

But a man will often have a little tussle with his conscience before doing what he wants to do but knows he ought not. Afterwards he may feel very uncomfortable about it. If so, he will probably make a big effort to convince himself that he's not such a bad fellow, really: after all, he will assure himself, there were some very special reasons for acting as he did. Sometimes, though not very often, he may try to put right the wrong he has done, simply to give himself some peace of mind.

This peculiar behaviour of man's is impossible to explain on an evolutionary basis. Glib statements by evolutionists that 'It comes about because man is a social animal' are only a way of obscuring the difficulty. They explain nothing. It is even arguable that the term 'social animal' ought not to be used at all, because it has such a wide range of meanings.

The biological social scale

The most social creatures of all are the social insects, like ants and bees. These live in such a co-operative way that they cannot possibly exist except in large communities. At the other extreme are non-social creatures like eagles or foxes, who need no company except that of a mate.

Between these two extremes is a more or less continuous scale, with various animals practising social living to different extents. Fairly close to the social insects are animals like wolves, which work together so closely that they would find it difficult to exist outside the pack. Nearer to the non-social end of the scale are birds like finches, which quite like going about in flocks but can get along perfectly happily on their own.

It is not easy to say exactly where man fits into this scale. A big city may look like an anthill, but in reality is nothing like it. City dwellers are not co-operating like ants; to a large extent they are in cut-throat competition with one another.

In any case, a big city is not man's natural environment. The members of a single family on an isolated sheep-farm in the mountains are living a more natural kind of life, and that is hardly a social environment at all. The most one can say about man, in the biological sense, is that he is a moderately social animal.

With non-social animals survival depends on self-help, and Darwinian theory says that such animals should evolve into thoroughly selfish creatures. In social animals the situation is rather different. A social animal could well benefit its relatives by sacrificing itself. In such circumstances a tendency towards instinctive unselfishness might possibly evolve.

'Might possibly' is the key phrase. This particular theory, which is based on a principle that biologists call 'kin selection through shared genes,' is one of the least plausible parts of the none-too-plausible theory of evolution. It is fraught with all sorts of ifs and buts.

For example, it is a waste of time, biologically speaking, for an animal to lay down its life for less than two brothers or eight cousins. (This is a consequence of Mendel's laws of inheritance.) For instinctive unselfishness to evolve, the overall benefits of an animal's sacrifice would have to outweigh the loss of its life. It is highly doubtful whether, in practice, this would generally be the case, because by sacrificing itself a social animal can only benefit its companions once, whereas by going on living it can benefit them time after time.

However, we can well afford to give this very shaky piece of evolutionary theory the benefit of the doubt and return to the problem of man's behaviour.

Man, the mixture

Perhaps *Homo sapiens* should really be classed as a non-social animal in the biological sense. If we do this, then Darwinism says he should have evolved into a totally selfish creature. Clearly, he has not done so.

On the other hand, if we follow the mainstream of biological thought and regard man as a more or less social animal, we have an equally big problem on our hands. Suppose that, for the sake of argument, we accept the dubious theory that kin selection can account for the evolution of unselfishness in social animals; then where does it lead us?

To the conclusion that man should have evolved into a thoroughly kind-hearted animal, who helps his fellow men as consistently as a wolf co-operates with the other members of his pack! It hardly needs saying that man is not a bit like that, either.

Instead, we find that *Homo sapiens* is a strange mixture. Although he would love to be always at peace within himself, his conflicting emotions are often as tangled as a pot of spaghetti. He admires qualities like self-sacrifice, kindness and compassion, and admits that men ought not to be selfish. Sometimes he manages to rise to great heights of selflessness, but most of his race spend most of their time living self-centred lives – while pretending to be much more unselfish than they really are.

No evolutionist has ever come to grips with this problem. Man's extraordinary moral sense, coupled with his contradictory moral behaviour, simply cannot be explained on any evolutionary basis.

There is only one explanation that comes anywhere near to fitting the facts, and that one fits perfectly. Man has a sense of right and wrong because there really are such things as right and wrong – absolute right and wrong[4] – and God made man capable of knowing the difference. But (as we saw in the previous chapter) man has perverted his own character by misusing the free will that God gave him. So he is constantly torn between what he wants to do, and what he knows he ought to do.

Why should an atheist be unselfish?

Man is an incurable idealist. All through history there have been many men and women ready to endure misery and even death for something they believed in. The ideals concerned were not always religious; men have suffered almost as much for political ideals, or even for art or the love of humanity.

To their credit, many atheists today are idealists. Yet they cannot explain why. They have no idea how the idealist urge could have evolved, since it is of no survival value, either to those individuals who possess it or to the human race as a whole.

They cannot even explain why they believe in being unselfish. I once asked a prominent member of the Humanist Society: 'Christians try to be unselfish for a very good reason: they believe that God has commanded them to do so. But since you don't believe in God, why do you believe in unselfishness?'

She replied: 'Because it makes me happy to be unselfish.'

156

I gave up at that. True, like most people I get a lot of inner satisfaction myself from doing good turns to people and seeing their appreciative faces. But I don't call that 'unselfishness'! Unselfishness, almost by definition, is doing something that makes you somewhat miserable because you think it is worth suffering a little to benefit somebody else.

Evidently, my humanist friend either did not know the meaning of the word unselfish, or did not have any explanation why she sometimes acts unselfishly – or both.

The only other reason I have known an unbeliever to give is this: 'We ought to be unselfish so as to benefit society as a whole.'

That sounds fine. But look at it closely, and you will see that it is another non-reason. 'Being unselfish' means 'benefiting other people in preference to ourselves'. 'Society as a whole' means 'other people'. So the unbeliever's stated reason boils down to this: 'We ought to benefit other people in preference to ourselves, so as to benefit other people.'

And what does that tell us? Precisely nothing. It is in the same street as the old song, 'King Charles he was King Charles he was, King Charles, he was King Charles ...'

So we have one more extraordinary fact about human nature. Many atheists *know* they ought to be unselfish; yet they have no idea *why* they ought to be.

How can that strange fact be explained? Only by recognising that we were created by a great Lawgiver, who created us with the ability to perceive that His laws are 'really right', and therefore ought to be obeyed.

The unsolved riddle

Although evolutionists have still not solved the riddle of our sense of right and wrong, it is not for the want of trying.

The eminent biologist C. H. Waddington made it the

157

most important part of his life's work. His book, *The Ethical Animal*,[5] now nearly twenty years old, is still probably the greatest work ever written on this subject. Yet, like the lesser writers who have followed him,[6] Waddington does not really offer a solution.

Admittedly, he offers a theory as to how we might have evolved our *capacity* to think in terms of right and wrong. This is a highly dubious theory, depending as it does on all sorts of unproved and questionable assumptions.

But he provides no answer at all to the really important question: how can we know whether our own ideas of right and wrong are correct – for example, how can we know that it is wrong to be greedy and selfish, and right to be generous and unselfish?

He faces up to the question and tries to answer it by considering the theory of evolution. Yet he admits to being baulked by one awkward fact: it is no use looking at the way things *are*, and assuming that that's the way they *ought* to be. For example, even if in nature we see 'the survival of the fittest' operating, that is no reason for us humans to behave like animals struggling for survival.

Strangely enough, nobody seems to have noticed this very obvious fact until the eighteenth century when the great philosopher Hume stated it in scholarly language.

Even more strangely, many people ignored Hume's warning and went on making the same silly mistake, right up to the middle of this century. H. G. Wells was one of them. He wrote: 'The world is no place for the bad, the stupid, the enervated. Their duty – it's a fine duty, too! – is to die. That is the path by which the beast rose to manhood, by which man goes on to higher things.'[7]

If Adolf Hitler ever read that he would have approved heartily. He used exactly the same sort of reasoning when he quoted Darwin as a justification for his gas chambers.

Most evolutionists are wiser nowadays. A few of them still seem to make the same dreadful mistake, but not many. Generally they agree – it is impossible to decide what is right and what is wrong by looking at the (supposed) evolutionary history of our planet.

Yet, having gone that far, they usually refuse to follow the argument any further, since the logical next step is too horrible to contemplate. As Bertrand Russell put it: 'If evolutionary ethics were sound, we ought to be entirely indifferent as to what the course of evolution may be.'[8]

Exactly. To be consistent, an elderly atheist ought to be able to say, 'I don't much care what happens to the human race in the next century, since I shan't be there to see it. If there is a nuclear holocaust and man goes the way of the dinosaurs, what does it matter? What's one more extinct species among millions?'

But unbelieving evolutionists are not consistent, fortunately. They do not talk like that. They know that there are certain things we ought to do, and that preserving the world for posterity is one of them.

They know these things, but they don't know how they know. Ask them: if evolution cannot advise us how we ought to behave, what can, unless we believe in God?

They have no answer.

Deep down in his heart the atheist probably knows that no answer is possible – that, unless there is a God, life just does not make sense.

Locked away in the deepest dungeon of every atheist's consciousness, I suspect, there is a believer waiting to be let out. After all, underneath his war-paint an atheist is still a creature made in God's own image.

Chapter 11

WHY CHRISTIANITY?

At this point we must turn to another question. The evidence marshalled in the previous ten chapters points to the existence of a Creator, but it does not indicate what sort of God that Creator is likely to be. Why, then, should we believe in the *Christian* God?

Why not Allah, the God of Mohammed? Or the gods of the Hindus, or of Lao-tse, or of any of the other Eastern religious teachers? Or could the world have been created by a God who is too high and mighty to have any further interest in our poor world? How can we be sure that God really is the loving Father that Jesus Christ declared Him to be?

Anything like a full reply to these questions would require a book to itself.[1] All I have room to do in this chapter is to take the first few steps along the road to an answer.

But first let us get one vital point clearly in mind. With one special exception which we shall come to shortly, Christianity is the only religion in the world that can defend itself by logical argument. I have sometimes asked believers in other religions, 'How can you prove to me that what you believe is likely to be true?' Invariably, they have not known how to reply.

Christianity is different. In any well-stocked Christian bookshop you will find a whole section labelled 'Christian Evidence' (or 'Apologetics', which means the same thing).[2] But you will not find many shelves full of books on 'Moslem Evidence', or 'Buddhist Evidence', or evidence for any other non-Christian religion. The few isolated books of this kind that do exist are only a feeble shadow of their Christian counterparts.

Recently I made this point while giving a seminar at a

university in California. Immediately a Jewish professor in the audience took me to task.

'How about the Jewish religion?' he demanded.

'A very good question,' I conceded. 'You are right – there is a great deal of evidence in support of the Jewish religion. But I don't regard the Jewish religion as something separate from Christianity. It is an incomplete version of the Christian faith.

'After all, four-fifths of the Christian Bible is the Jewish Bible, which Christians call the Old Testament. Consequently, any evidence that the Old Testament is a message from God is evidence in favour of both Jewish and Christian religions alike.'

This is important because there are two especially powerful lines of evidence in favour of Christianity. First, there are the indications that God has long been overruling human history; secondly, there is the evidence that He is at work through Jesus Christ. And the first of these proofs has a great deal to do with the Jews.

God produces His evidence

There have always been different opinions on what lies behind world history.

One idea is that the world has just drifted along – in other words, that human society as we know it today has just evolved. The other view is that an unseen God has been quietly shaping human history: as one Old Testament prophet, Daniel, put it: 'The Most High rules the kingdom of men, and gives it to whom he will.'[3]

Which of these two explanations best fits the facts?

It might be difficult to decide, were it not for one thing. *God has decided to use the Jews as evidence of His work in the world*. Hundreds of years before Christ was born, God said:

Thus says the Lord, he who created you, O Jacob,
  He who formed you, O Israel,

161

'Fear not for I have redeemed you,
    I have called you by name, you are mine . . .'
Let all the nations gather together,
    And let the peoples assemble.
Who among them can declare this,
    And show us the former things?
Let them bring their witnesses to justify them,
    And let them hear and say, It is true.
'*You* [Israel] *are my witnesses*', says the Lord.[4]

With a modern lawcourt scene in mind, perhaps it
would be better not to describe the Jews by Isaiah's word,
'witnesses', because 'exhibits' would probably be a more
accurate description nowadays. They are in the same category as, say, the photographs of mutilated victims which
might be produced in a cruelty trial, as evidence that certain events have taken place. The history of Israel is one
big collection of exhibits, all of them indicating that the
God of Israel has been at work amongst His people.

Strange history

However you look at it, there can be no denying that the
Jews have had an extraordinary history.

In their early days they were an insignificant little
nation. Their tiny country was rather like Belgium – a
natural battlefield, uncomfortably sandwiched between
great powers. Because of this they were rarely free of
invading armies for more than a few years at a time. Such
independence as they ever possessed was precarious and
rather short-lived.

Within about a hundred years of Jesus Christ's death
their land was twice devastated by the Romans. Each
time great numbers were sold into slavery in foreign
lands, and on the second occasion every last Jew was
banished from the Jewish heartland, Judea.

From then until modern times the Jews were a nation
without a homeland. There has never been another

nation with a record like theirs. Every other nation sub-
jected to that sort of treatment has died out long ago. Yet
somehow the Jews succeeded in surviving eighteen long
centuries of exile, of universal dislike, of rejection and
persecution and attempted genocide.

How did they manage it? Historians do not really
know. They can only accept that somehow, despite everything and everybody, the Jews have come through. But
how?

Unbelievers have concocted all sorts of theories in an
effort to explain the Jews' strange ability to survive. None
of them is convincing. The trouble is that the survival of
the Jews is little short of miraculous – and it is very hard
for an unbeliever to explain a miracle convincingly.

History written before it happened

In the Old Testament passage quoted above, God threw
out a challenge. He dared the ungodly nations to produce
their own evidence, and said that Israel would be His
evidence. Now here are two more Old Testament verses
where God challenges the world.

> Surely the Lord God does nothing, without revealing
> his secret to his servants the prophets.[5]

> When a prophet speaks in the name of the Lord, if the
> word does not come to pass or come true, that is a
> word which the Lord has not spoken.[6]

In other words, God declared that He would reveal His
intentions through the prophets, before causing certain
events to occur. And God suggested an easy test for
doubtful readers to apply: bogus prophets would be
unable to foretell the future accurately; only God Himself, speaking through genuine prophets, can do that.

Judged by that test the Old Testament is staggeringly
successful. In dozens and dozens of places it clearly fore-
told the astonishing history of the Jews – and did so

hundreds of years before it happened. Here is just one example out of many:

> You shall become a horror, a proverb, and a byword, among all the peoples where the Lord will lead you away ... You shall be plucked off the land which you are entering to take possession of it. And the Lord will scatter you among all peoples, from one end of the earth to the other ... And among these nations you shall find no ease, and there shall be no rest for the sole of your foot.[7]

And that is exactly the way it has been.

The Bible said the Jews would all be expelled from their homeland – and they were.

The Bible said the Jews would not just be removed into some other country, but scattered all over the world – and they were.

The Bible said the Jews would have a miserable time in the days of their exile – and right up till the end of World War II that's how it was with them.

The challenge that Hitler accepted

The Bible has thrown out yet another challenge concerning the Jews to the world. Several times it said that the Jews would never be allowed to die out – that they would, in fact, outlive their persecutors. Here is one such prophecy:

> Fear not, O Jacob [the Jews] my servant, says the Lord,
> For I am with you.
> I will make a full end of all the nations to which I have driven you,
> *But of you I will not make a full end.*[8]

Adolf Hitler was mad enough to take up that challenge. He thought he was powerful enough to conquer the world and destroy the entire Jewish people. Before his lunatic career ended he had murdered some six million Jews.

But the Bible's promise was upheld. There was made a 'full end' of Hitler and his Reich, which he vainly thought would last a thousand years. And the small Jewish race lives on, as great a force in world affairs as ever.

Although Hitler was the most spectacular, he was by no means the only would-be exterminator of the Jews. Through most of their long exile somebody, somewhere, has been trying to get rid of them, either by massacre or by expulsion. And again and again the result has been the same: the Jews have survived, while their persecutors have passed away.

This has all happened exactly as the Bible said it would happen. It is extremely difficult to explain the Bible's uncanny foresight unless we accept the Bible's own explanation – that the God of the Bible has been at work, keeping His promises to the Jews.

Homecoming

Within living memory a remarkable change in Jewish fortune has taken place. After eighteen hundred years without a land to call their own, a mere handful of Jews have achieved the near-impossible.

By all the ordinary rules of history the State of Israel ought not to exist. Indeed, as recently as 1947 it did not exist, and a mere half-century before then there were only a few thousand Jews in the Holy Land. At the time of writing, many Arabs still refuse to recognise officially that Israel does exist, and would like to wipe it off the map.

And the Arab nations possess most of the trump cards. They have something like a hundred times Israel's population, and superiority in planes, tanks, guns, and nearly everything else with which to wage war. They possess the greatest part of the non-Communist world's oil, and that gives the Arabs enormous power and international influence in a world which is running out of sources of cheap energy.

Yet despite all the odds stacked against her, little Israel survives. She has fought four wars in a quarter of a century, and emerged bloody but unbowed each time.

As with the Jews over the centuries, so with the State of Israel today, there is one great question demanding a solution: how have they managed it? And once again there is the same clear answer: only with the help of some Power greater than themselves.

Israel's fantastic achievements were not unexpected to those who know the Bible. Many an Old Testament prophecy declared that it would be so. For instance:

He who scattered Israel will gather him,
And will keep him as a shepherd keeps his flock.
For the Lord has ransomed Jacob [the Jews]
   And has redeemed him from hands too strong for him.[9]

A nation of unbelievers

Surprising though it may seem, most of the Israelis fulfilling these prophecies are blind to the real facts. They give little credit to God for 'redeeming Israel from hands too strong for him'. Instead, they arrogantly ascribe their successes to their own nerve and skill.

Sadly, the nation of Israel, by and large, no longer believes in the God of Israel. As the Jewish writer, Herman Wouk, has put it:

Israel is not a religious country, in the accepted sense ... The land of Israel, the new fulfilment of the most ancient religious dream on earth, was conceived by an irreligious founder and brought into being by men for the most part not observers of the faith ... it is less than realistic to think of Israel at the moment as anything but a virile little secular nation.[10]

166

And this, too, is exactly as the Bible said it would be.
Here are the words of another prophet, foretelling the
eventual return of Israel to their ancient land:

> Thus says the Lord God: It is not for your sake, O
> house of Israel that I am about to act, but for the sake
> of my holy name *which you have profaned* among the
> nations . . . I will take you from the nations, and gather
> you from all the countries and bring you into your own
> land . . . Then you will remember your evil ways, and
> your deeds that were not good; *and you will loathe
> yourselves for your iniquities and your abominable
> deeds.* It is not for your sake that I will act, says the
> Lord God.[11]

The meaning of these words of the Bible is un-
mistakable. They are highly unflattering to the Jews, and
this makes it all the more remarkable that they appear in
the Jewish national book. They told the world of 500 BC
that when the nation of Israel at last came to be reborn, it
would consist largely of ungodly Jews. And as anyone
can see, the prophecy has come true in our own time.

Another interesting feature of this prophecy is the
reference to the Jews 'loathing themselves' for their un-
godliness. This implies that, eventually, they will have a
change of heart. But as other prophecies indicate, that
will not occur until the time of their Messiah's return.

Meanwhile, Israel – poor, courageous, brilliant, self-
reliant, cocksure, conceited, unbelieving Israel – remains
what the Jews have always been: a living proof that the
God of Israel is.

The hub of world history

Even if these facts stood alone they would form a powerful case for believing in the God of the Bible. But in fact
they form only a tiny fraction of the Bible-based evidence that God is still active in human affairs.

For although He has a special interest in Israel, God is

167

concerned with all the other nations, too. The relation between Israel and the rest of the world is stated like this in an early book of the Bible:

> When the Most High gave to the nations their
>   inheritance,
>   When he separated the children of men,
> He set the bounds of the peoples
>   According to the number of the children of Israel.[12]

This suggests that God intended Israel to play some kind of key role in world history. There can be no doubt that the Jews have indeed had an enormous influence on world affairs. In particular, there was one period when the whole future course of history revolved around Israel.

In the first century AD the nation of Israel not only cradled Jesus Christ; Israel also mothered Christianity itself. Without a nucleus of God-fearing Jews in the Holy Land, the Christian faith would have lacked a home base. Equally important, the presence of Jewish communities all over the Roman Empire provided seedbeds for Christianity in every civilised land.

So, for several reasons, Christianity would never have been born had it not been for the Jews of nineteen centuries ago. And without Christianity human history would have been very different indeed.

Israel and the twentieth-century crisis

Once more the world stands at a great crossroads. And it looks as though Israel is about to play a central role once more in events that will shape the whole world's destiny.

From beginning to end the Bible talks of a supreme climax to human history. In the Old Testament this is related to the appearance of a great leader called 'Messiah'. The New Testament frequently refers to the same event as the second coming of Jesus Christ.

168

In both testaments the great occurrence is said to be connected with two other unique events. The first of these was to be the long-awaited return of Israel to their own country. The other was a state of great distress over all the earth – 'a time of trouble, such as never has been since there was a nation till that time', as Daniel 12:1 puts it.

Jesus Christ linked them both with his own return to the earth in Luke 21. He listed the following events which had to take place, in this order:

(1) The destruction of Jerusalem, which happened in AD 70 (vv. 20–3).

(2) The exile of the Jews, which began in AD 70, was made total in AD 135, and remained almost complete until the twentieth century (v. 24a).

(3) The return of Israel to the ancient city of Jerusalem, which occurred in 1967 (v. 24b).

(4) What Christ called 'distress of nations in perplexity ... men fainting with fear and foreboding of what is coming on the world' (vv. 25 and 26).

(5) His return: 'Then they will see the Son of man coming in a cloud with power and great glory' (v. 27).

Black future

Already (3) has taken place, and (4) is looming up ahead. We may not quite have reached the stage of 'men fainting with fear and foreboding of what is coming on the world' yet. But that is only because most of us can't see further ahead than the day after tomorrow. Men whose job it is to study the way the world is going[13] tell us that by the year 2000 the world is likely to have:

- Over six thousand million people in it – half of them practically starving.
- Permanent famines in dozens of countries.
- Desperate shortages of oil and other sources of energy.

169

- Equally severe shortages of fertilisers and of several vitally important metals.
- Many small countries in possession of atomic bombs.
- The three superpowers armed with horrifying new weapons that could destroy all life on earth a hundred times over.

There can be no doubt that human history is racing towards some appalling cataclysm. The one bright spot in a dark picture is the way the Bible has clearly foreseen our twentieth-century problems – and that is a very bright spot indeed.

No other sacred book offers any evidence that God is still in full control of His world. The Bible, and only the Bible, gives good reason for thinking that God will do what man cannot do – act decisively, to save human society from total collapse and ruin.

That is our first reason for believing that the Being who created this superb universe is the God of Christianity.

Chapter 12

FILLING THE GOD-SHAPED HOLE

The second answer to the question, Why Christianity?, can be stated in one word: Christ.

Christianity is not 'just another religion'. It is in a class of its own, just as its Founder was.

This was brought home forcibly to a young missionary preparing for work in India, when he asked an ex-missionary, 'Whatever shall I say to the Hindus when they start singing the praises of their own religion, which I don't fully understand?'

'Simple,' replied the older man. 'Don't get involved in an argument with them. Just ask them what is their remedy for sin. You will find they don't have one. And neither does any other religion, except Christianity!'

He was right, even if he did overstate his case a little. Other religious leaders may have provided good moral teachings, and advice on prayer, worship, and other religious activities. But Christ went much further; He, and He alone, has provided a complete and final solution to the problems of human weakness and human wickedness. Every other prophet has stopped short of that.

Baha'u'llah, the last person to found a world religion, can be regarded as fairly typical. This nineteenth-century preacher wrote: 'The real treasure of man is his knowledge. Knowledge is the means of honour, prosperity, joy, gladness, happiness and exultation.'[1]

One of his present-day followers, the American, William Sears, has summarised the views of Baha'is on education thus:

In the Faith of Baha'u'llah, the fundamental importance and limitless possibilities of education are proclaimed in the clearest terms. When education on the right lines becomes general, humanity will be transformed, and the world will become a paradise.[2]

What a hope! With man the fallen, warped, blundering creature that he is, it will obviously take something more than 'education on the right lines' to transform this world into a paradise.

Jesus Christ, alone among the world's religious leaders, offers man the extra something that he needs.

Inner space

Bertrand Russell was one of the great thinkers of the modern age. Yet in some ways he was a pathetic figure. An avowed atheist, with no time for Christian morality, he turned to one activity after another (and one woman after another) in a vain quest for happiness.

Those who knew him best found it hard to decide what Russell was really seeking. His daughter, Katharine Tait, has made a most revealing comment in a recently published biography of her father: 'Somewhere at the back of my father's mind, at the bottom of his heart, in the depths of his soul, there was an empty space that had once been filled by God and he never found anything else to put in it.'[3]

What! A God-shaped hole? Inside Bertrand Russell, of all people?

At first sight his daughter's conclusion seems preposterous. But the more you think about it, the more reasonable it seems.

Man – any man, every man, and every woman, too – is a restless creature at heart. We are all born revolutionaries, with an itch to change things for the better. It may be the government, or the local Women's Institute, or the way Father picks his teeth – you name it, we all have an urge to improve something or someone, somewhere.

172

But these targets for our reforming zeal are only a blind. Deep down, we know where the real inadequacy lies: in ourselves, as much as in our fellows.

More than anything else we crave for things like love, and joy, and peace. We want to see more patience, kindness, goodness, faithfulness, gentleness and self-control. But we never seem to find nearly enough of them, either in others or (come on, let's admit it) in ourselves. Those qualities seem nearly as elusive as the immortality that most people also hanker after.

This makes another fine problem for unbelievers and evolutionists. The animals only desire things that can be had, like food, and warmth, and sex, and rest. Then how did the human race develop a deep-seated desire for so many unattainable objects? The unbelievers have no satisfactory explanation to offer.

But the Bible has. It says that those delightful moral qualities mentioned above are not unattainable – except to people who seek them in the wrong way. It brackets them together as what it calls 'the fruit of the Spirit'.[4] They *can* be made to grow within us, but only by the power of God's Spirit. This comes to man on God's terms, we are told, and that means through Christ and by the influence of His Word.[5]

Many generations of believers have found for themselves that this is no empty promise.

Meeting man's deepest needs

Evidently, the emptiness in man's restless soul is both God-given and God-shaped, even though many of us cannot see it so. And Jesus Christ is exactly the right size and shape to fill that aching void.

This is the vital difference between Christianity and all other religions. Take Buddhism, for instance. Buddhists believe that their founder ceased to exist[6] when his work on earth was finished. All that matters is the teaching he

173

left behind. So with the other great religious teachers: whether they still exist or not is of little consequence – all that really counts is their teaching.

But if Jesus Christ had passed away, His teaching – superb though it is – would be as lifeless as a car without an engine. His word has power, in a way that no other religious teacher's word has. Why? Because His followers believe Him to be alive and actively working on their behalf.

This highlights another great difference between Christianity and the rest. There are miracle-stories connected with most religions. But in all the others the miracles are optional extras, like car radios and rear window wipers: you can leave them out, if you like, and still have much the same religion left.

Only Christianity has the miraculous element built into its very foundations. A non-miraculous Christianity would be only a feeble travesty of the religion that Christ founded. This becomes evident as soon as we take a studied look at the character of its Founder.

Lunatic – or Son of God?

There were two views of Jesus of Nazareth amongst those who knew Him personally.

On the one hand were His friends. They called Him, 'the Christ, the Son of the living God,'[7] or even, 'My Lord and my God!'[8]

On the other were those who rejected Him. They called Him both mad and bad: a man who was both possessed of the devil[9] and in league with the devil.[10] Above all they accused Him of blasphemy.[11]

There was no middle ground between those two extremes; it was one thing or the other in those days. There were no unbelieving Jews then who deigned to say, as the modern Jewish novelist, Sholem Asch, has said: 'Jesus Christ is the outstanding personality of all time . . . every act and word of Jesus has value for all of us. He became

174

the Light of the World. Why shouldn't I, a Jew, be proud of that?'

Nor was there then any unbelieving Gentile prepared to admit, as the atheist Lord Boothby has condescendingly admitted: 'I believe the teachings of Jesus are the best that have been offered to mankind.'

It is handsome of Asch and Boothby, as non-Christians, to honour Jesus as the greatest religious teacher of all time. Handsome – but very foolish. The first-century unbelievers were much more sensible. Any man who claimed *falsely* to be the Son of God would indeed have been a blasphemous lunatic. The only possible alternative was that Jesus' claims were true: that He really was the Son of God. There were no people taking the middle ground in those days, for the simple reason that there was not – and still is not – any middle ground to take.

Here is a short selection of the claims He made.

I am the Son of God.[12]

I and the Father are one.[13]

He (God) has not left me alone, for I always do what is pleasing to him.[14]

Which of you convicts me of sin?[15]

I lay down my life that I may take it again ... I have power to take it again.[16]

The Son of man will be delivered into the hands of men, and they will kill him; and when he is killed, after three days he will rise.[17]

This is my blood of the covenant, which is poured out for many for the forgiveness of sins.[18]

I am leaving the world and going to the Father.[19]

Hereafter you will see the Son of man seated at the right hand of power, and coming on the clouds of heaven.[20]

When the Son of man comes in his glory, and all the

angels with him, then will he sit on his glorious throne. Before him will be gathered all the nations . . .[21]

As the Father has life in himself, so he has granted the Son also to have life in himself . . . the hour is coming when all who are in the tombs will hear his voice and come forth.[22]

A living miracle

We can summarise the claims that Jesus made like this. He said He was:

(1) The Son of God.
(2) Sinless.
(3) Able to free us from our sins by His death.
(4) Destined to rise from His grave.
(5) And to ascend into heaven.
(6) Afterwards to return to the earth in glory.
(7) Then to raise the dead, and judge them.

Either those claims were true, or they were false.

If they were true, it means that Jesus was a super-human being, a living miracle. Many people find this hard to believe.

But what is the alternative? If those claims of His had been false, it would follow that Jesus, who was admittedly the greatest moral teacher the world has ever known, must also have been the craziest megalomaniac in all history! And that is very much harder to believe.

There is no escape from these two alternatives. There just is no other possibility. In particular, it is no use suggesting that Jesus spoke only those parts of the Gospel which contain His moral teaching, while other men, later on, added the hundreds of verses containing His astonishing claims.

The Gospels are too ancient for that. Modern studies have shown that at least three of the Gospels were written well within the lifetime of the young men who heard

Jesus preach, and the fourth was in existence soon after.[23] With so many eyewitnesses around them, the writers of the Gospels would never have got away with a gross perversion of the facts.

Tricksters are not heroes

In any case, why should the Gospel writers have wanted to distort the facts?

The early Christians gained nothing material out of their religion. First the Jews and then the Romans persecuted them and tried to suppress their activities. The more they preached, the more they were likely to suffer the loss of livelihood, beating, imprisonment and death.

These men's sacrifice did not prove them to be right, of course, since history is full of the stories of brave men who were mistaken. What it did prove was their sincerity. The men who knew Jesus personally must surely have believed that He really made those tremendous claims.

More than that, they obviously believed that the claims were justified. They not only believed that He *claimed* to be sinless; they believed that He *was* sinless. And since some of them lived with Him for months at a time, they had ample opportunity to verify that particular claim.

Similarly, they not only believed that He *claimed* He would rise from the dead and ascend to heaven; they believed that He actually did so.

Indeed, they took pains to tell their readers, time after time, that they *knew* Jesus rose from the grave. As Luke put it, 'He presented himself alive after his passion by many proofs.'[24]

They met many people who said to them, 'A crucified man rose from the grave? What an absurd tale! You must have been dreaming.'

To which they replied, in effect, 'Yes, that's just what we thought ourselves at first. We simply couldn't believe our eyes. The first disciple to see the risen Lord thought it

177

must be the gardener,[25] and two others mistook Him for a total stranger.[26]

'When He first appeared to a whole group of us, we all thought we were seeing things. It never occurred to us that this really was Jesus, brought back to life again. So He told us to touch Him and satisfy ourselves that He was really there. That still wasn't enough for us, so He asked for some food and ate it before our eyes.[27] After that we just had to face the fact!

'Even that was not all. He was with us for several weeks, on and off, teaching us many things we needed to know.[28] You don't think we all imagined that, do you?'

Christ's enemies were not fools

In the time of Jesus Christ the religious leaders of the Jews were a poor lot, in the main. Only a few were willing to be taught, and those few had to watch their step.[29] Some were genuine enough, but were thoroughly entrenched in their mistaken beliefs.[30]

Many were thoroughgoing hypocrites, who had turned religion into a moneymaking racket.[31] These were the men who had Christ crucified, and who afterwards did all in their power to suppress Christianity. But as history has shown, they were unsuccessful. Though they did their best to kill it, the new religion flourished exceedingly.

Their dismal failure is powerful evidence that Christ was what He claimed to be.

These men were no fools. They were ruthless schemers, used to playing power politics. They would have destroyed Christianity at a stroke if only they could have undermined its foundations. Yet they failed to do so. Why?

Why did they not say, 'That Jesus of yours is not sinless. Far from it: here is a long list of sins He is known to have committed.'? That catalogue of Christ's sins would have been worth a king's ransom to them. If Jesus had been an ordinary man – even an outstandingly good man – it would have been easy to have compiled such a list. Yet they never managed to produce one. Why?

Nor did they say, 'Jesus never rose from the dead – look, here is His dead body!' A public display of that corpse would have destroyed Christianity at its birth – and yet the arch-enemies of the Christian faith never succeeded in producing it. Why?

Instead, they put out a cock-and-bull story about a handful of demoralised disciples stealing the body from under the noses of a guard of picked troops – and all despite the close personal attention being given to the affair by the Roman governor and the savage Jewish ruling class. Christ's enemies really must have had their backs to the wall, if that was the best excuse they could concoct.

Those Jewish rulers were powerful, determined men. They won Round One decisively when they crucified Christ and His disciples all ran away. Yet in Round Two those rulers were utterly routed, and the formerly timid disciples began, with hearts like lions, to turn the whole world upside down. Whatever happened between the two rounds, to turn the tables so completely?

Only one answer makes any sense.

God must have worked a mighty miracle, by raising Jesus Christ from the dead.

The ring of truth

Many an unbeliever has been converted through reading the Gospels. Those four short books possess a most extraordinary property: the more closely you look at them, the more they seem to ring true.

The miracle stories, for instance, seem incredible when you first encounter them. But after a while they begin to fit naturally into place. They are in complete accord with Christ's tremendous claims: you might have expected that the Son of God, the Creator, would use His Father's power at times to benefit suffering humanity.

179

His miraculous birth from a virgin may also seem strange at first but only until you ponder the significance of His sinlessness, and His claim to be God's Son. Then it fits neatly into place. Could there be any better introduction to a 'virgin life' – that is to say, a life of utter selflessness and perfection – than a virgin birth? What better way could there be of demonstrating to mankind that this Man was, *literally*, the Son of God?

Then again, in what better way could God show the depth of His love to the world than by allowing men to murder His Son? And afterwards what could be more fitting than for God, the Creator of every living thing, to restore His Son's body to life again?

The story of Jesus Christ's days on earth is not a disjointed collection of speeches and events. It is one superb sequence of words and deeds, harmonising together like the many different instruments in a full orchestra. And this is despite the existence of four separate Gospels, each with its own view of Christ.

The resulting picture of Jesus is so realistic that He almost seems to step out of the pages of the New Testament as a living man.

This is why Jesus is so real to His followers today. Other religious leaders are teachers, and that is all. But Jesus is very much more than that. To His disciples He is teacher, *and* friend, *and* example, *and* rescuer, *and* priest, *and* king.

Christ is real

There is a simple rule of conduct taught in nearly every Christian school: when in doubt, always ask yourself, 'What would Jesus do?'

It works with five-year-olds and with university professors. Prime ministers and presidents have been known to go by it. But it would never have been so popular but for one thing: Jesus Christ is a real person to those who know the Gospels. And He is a person who really does meet every human need.

You don't find philosophers running their lives by the question, What would Socrates do? Or young Conservatives by, What would Churchill do? Nobody ever seems to ask, What would Lenin, or Abe Lincoln, or Confucius, or Napoleon, do?

No, it is only, What would Jesus do? Men know that it wouldn't work with anyone else. Jesus is different.

Jesus is *real*.

And Jesus supplies the answer to our needs – every time.

Christ at work today

Jesus Christ once described His method of working like this: "Behold, I stand at the door and knock; if any one hears my voice and opens the door, I will come in to him.'[32]

He spoke those words after He rose from the dead and became all-powerful. Obviously, He does not need to stand waiting. Even if we barricade it, He could batter the door down in a moment if He wished. But He makes it plain that He will not walk in uninvited, not even if He finds the door ajar.

He makes the first move: He comes to the door and knocks. Then it is up to us to respond. If we don't, He will go away and try some other person's door.

This is why He has had so many apparent failures. But they are not really His failures, any more than the patients who pour their medicines down the kitchen sink can be regarded as a doctor's failures.

We must judge Him by the results He has with those who say, 'Come in,' and really mean it. And by that yardstick He has a fantastic record of success.

His effect on the Auca Indians of Ecuador deserves to be even more widely known than it is. Until a generation ago, these stone-age tribesmen in a remote corner of the

181

South American jungle were almost unbelievably ferocious. Killing each other was such a way of life with them that very few of their males ever grew middle-aged. Understandably, the rest of the world left them severely alone.

In 1956 five young missionaries kissed their wives and children goodbye and went to live in an Auca village, where no white man had ever lived before. Within a few days they were all speared to death.

After the shock of bereavement had worn off, some of the widows went to live in the same Auca village, determined to carry on where their murdered husbands had left off.

Gradually the Aucas became impressed by the love and selflessness, and above all by the forgiving spirits, of the bereaved women. Within a few years several of the killers and many other Aucas accepted the religion of the men they had murdered. The formerly violent tribe grew peaceful, and Aucas began to visit nearby tribes as missionaries, urging their savage neighbours to find a better life through Christ.

This is no isolated tale. Wherever and whenever men have *really* taken the Christian message (or even a substantial part of it) to their hearts, love and peace have triumphed joyfully over all that is worst in man.

No other religion can claim a great multitude of peaceful victories over violence and evil. There is something very, very special about the power of Jesus Christ.

The last word

The final say is bound to be yours. Sooner or later we all have to decide for ourselves about God.

A book like this can do no more than marshal facts. It can list the reasons for believing that God is, and that Jesus Christ is His Son. What it cannot do is to impart faith, because that, the New Testament tells us, comes from the Word of God[33].

But the facts are a sound foundation on which to base one's faith. Let's think back over the facts we have looked at in this book.

The first three chapters cleared the ground. The myth that belief is no longer reasonable in this scientific age was exploded. There are lots of unbelieving scientists, it is true – but lots of believing scientists as well.

In chapter 4 we looked at an almost unbelievable collection of 'coincidences', without which life in this universe, and especially on Planet Earth, would be impossible.

Chapter 5 noted that biologists do not know how the first living things and the first primitive cells could have been formed. In the light of recent discoveries, the origin of life looks more like a miracle than ever it did. All the evidence, in fact, suggests that it *was* a miracle.

The next two chapters provided a great many reasons for thinking that living things were planned, designed, created, rather than being the product of natural forces. In many ways, Nature seems to 'think ahead', to know where she is going, to have an ultimate purpose in mind. This all provides very good grounds for believing in a Creator.

We looked at *Homo sapiens* in chapter 8. Anything less like a product of evolution would be hard to imagine. The evidence shouts at us that man is not an ape on the way up, but a creature in God's image who has fallen down.

In chapter 9 we digressed, to deal with a number of objections to belief, like the problem of evil. None of them proved too great a difficulty.

Chapter 10 considered man's moral faculties. We saw that evolutionists are all at sea over this: despite strenuous efforts, they cannot begin to explain how mankind's recognition of certain things as 'right', and other things as 'wrong', could possibly have evolved.

There was space in chapter 11 for only a tiny fraction of the case for believing the Bible to be a message from

God. We concentrated on the Jews as evidence that God has been at work in history – a line of argument which is backed by more than two thousand years of fulfilled prophecies.

Finally, in this chapter, we have looked at a few of the reasons for believing that Jesus Christ is the Son of God. Here, also, the facts seem to point inevitably towards belief.

The pull of the familiar

Yes, you will probably admit, it all adds up to a plausible case. And yet – and yet . . .

And yet, what? It isn't a watertight case? That's no reason for brushing it under the carpet. None of the great decisions in life is based on a watertight case. You chose your career, or your wife, or a place to live, on the basis of a mere handful of facts. By comparison, you have an enormous mass of facts on which to base your choice of a religious belief.

No, it isn't the lack of evidence that's bothering you. Logic probably plays only a very small part in your reactions at this stage. Your instinctive, 'Yes, but . . .', is born of another urge – the desire to hold on to the old, the secure, the familiar.

In the slums of any of our big cities you can find children growing up on a pathetic diet of bread and cakes and chips and sweets. As any welfare worker will tell you, trying to get them to switch to healthier meals is a thankless task. They do not realise that they are not being properly nourished; they want to stick to the foods they know.

For years and years you have been filling that God-shaped hole inside you with starchy substitutes for God. *Of course* you don't want to change. You're comfortable enough as you are. But you have no idea how much better off you would be if you threw out the substitutes and took God on board.

Most of us have met heavy smokers who say, 'I'd give it up tomorrow if I thought the evidence was conclusive. But I'm not convinced that it does cause cancer.'

And we feel sorry for them, for it is so painfully obvious that they are deceiving themselves. There is no question about the evidence that smoking is bad for you, in all sorts of ways. The real problem is that they are hooked on nicotine. Quibbling about the evidence is just a rationalisation, an excuse.

It is like that with most unbelievers today, who may think they have an intellectual problem connected with science, or history, or the lack of logical proof. But such things are only camouflage. The real difficulty is much deeper.

Their trouble is that they are hooked on unbelief.

The way forward

A few days ago I was talking to a middle-aged seaman. He was not an educated man, but he had more sense, more real wisdom, than many a university professor. Until a couple of years ago he had been a lifelong unbelief-addict. Quietly he explained how he had broken free.

'I became impressed with the evidence that there is a God. But something kept pulling me back. I couldn't quite accept it, but I couldn't forget it, either. My mind was in turmoil.

'Then, one night, I found the way out. I went down on my knees and said, "O God, if you do exist, please – please – take charge of my life!" '

'And then what happened?' I asked.

'Well – He just did!'

Not every prayer of that kind is answered as swiftly as this man's evidently was. Often it takes months, or even years, of searching, of praying, of reading the Bible. But the answer, clear and definite, always comes in the end.

We may be sure of that. The Lord Jesus Christ has given us His word for it:

185

Ask, and it will be given you; seek, and you will find; knock, and it will be opened to you. For every one who asks receives, and he who seeks finds, and to him who knocks it will be opened.[34]

Appendix

CHRISTIAN VIEWS OF CREATION

All Christians are agreed that God is the Creator of the universe. But they are not by any means agreed on what they mean by the word, 'Creator'. There are many different views on how God may have carried out the work of creation, but there is only space here to discuss the most widely held ones. I shall reserve to the last the theory that, to my mind, best fits both the scientific facts and the requirements of Scripture.

Theistic evolution

Theistic evolution is probably the most popular view of creation in intellectual circles. It is based on the philosophy, 'If you can't beat the atheistic evolutionists, join them!' and it runs something like this.

God created matter and took infinite pains to endow it with exactly the right properties. So matter contained within itself the potential to advance along a course mapped out by God. All He then needed to do was to give an initial push (such as the 'big bang' astronomers talk about) and then let evolution follow its predetermined path.

That is the basic theory, but like most theories it is capable of popping up in a number of slightly different forms. Some theistic evolutionists, for instance, hold that God did more than start the process going – He needed to inject divine power into it from time to time, to keep it moving on the right lines.

The variations on the theme are unimportant, however. The essential feature of theistic evolution is a belief that evolution has occurred, but that God and not blind chance was behind it.

187

To my mind, this view is like a lot of fashionable schools of thought – superficially attractive, but open to a number of serious objections when you look at it closely.

First of all, it is based upon a misconception of where evolutionary theory stands today. In reality the question of 'joining them because we can't beat them' does not arise. Evolution remains what it has always been – an interesting but highly speculative idea, open to very serious objections, and by no means universally accepted amongst biologists.

Moreover, theistic evolution is not at all a good fit to the scientific data. As we saw in chapter 6, nature is full of gaps. There are frequently big gaps between living species, even bigger gaps in the fossil record, and positively enormous gaps between a great many elaborate organs and the primitive organs which are supposed to have preceded them. If the Creator had employed a continuous evolutionary process, we should expect to find smooth transitions everywhere, not a multitude of gaps.

Theistic evolutionists are generally inclined to treat the Bible with less respect than it deserves. Although Genesis 1 is not free from problems, one thing stands out clearly: it speaks of a series of distinct acts of creation, and not one long continuous process. And it is hard to reconcile Christ's teaching about Genesis with theistic evolution, unless you say (as some theistic evolutionists have said) that Christ was a child of the times in which He lived, and consequently was wrong in His view of the Old Testament.

Because evolution is the kingpin of modern atheism, a heavy price has been paid for the concessions that the theistic evolutionists have made. A belief in theistic evolution has proved for many one-time Christians to be a stepping-stone to unbelief.

Biblical literalism

Biblical literalism stands at the opposite extreme from theistic evolution. Unfortunately, we live in days when extremists of all kinds seem to flourish, and there has recently been a remarkable revival of literalism.

Respect for the text of the Old Testament is a very good and necessary thing. The Lord Jesus Christ always treated it as authoritative, and that is a very good reason for us to do the same.

But the literalist, though he has the best of intentions, goes too far. He has an unfortunate tendency to pull verses out of their context in the Bible and give them a literal meaning, regardless of whether they were intended to be read that way. This often results in highly dubious interpretations of the Bible, and sometimes in outright confusion.

The twenty-sixth chapter of the Book of Job supplies a couple of illustrations. Verse 11 says:

> The pillars of heaven tremble,
> And are astounded at his [God's] rebuke.

Not so very long ago literalists used to quote that as a 'proof' that the earth is flat and heaven a canopy over it, held up by enormous pillars. Then the Flat Earth Society fell out of favour, and literalists switched their attention from verse 11 to verse 7, which says:

> He [God] stretches out the north over the void,
> And hangs the earth upon nothing.

I have seen that verse quoted in several fairly recent books as a 'proof' that the Bible was way ahead of Copernicus, Galileo and Newton. To these literalist writers the verse teaches that the earth is suspended in empty space by invisible forces. Needless to say, these books carefully avoided mentioning that another verse nearby appears to teach the opposite!

The truth is, of course, that the Book of Job is a magnificent piece of poetry. Like all great poems, it is alive with vivid figures of speech. To take this figurative language literally, or to use Job as if it were meant to be a textbook on astronomy, is far from wise.

When it comes to the creation story in Genesis, today's literalists are not always consistent in their literalism. The Bible says that the sun, moon and stars were not created until the fourth day of creation, after the creation of day and night (Day 1) and vegetation (Day 3).

The current fashion amongst some literalists is to say that this, at least, is not literal. They usually suggest – not unreasonably – that the 'creation' of sun, moon and stars was really their first appearance from the standpoint of an observer on earth; as the earth cooled down the thick clouds above it would have thinned out, until eventually the heavenly bodies could be seen for the first time.

It is a pity that all literalists do not exercise the same kind of discretion when it comes to the six days of creation. Instead, they generally insist that these must have been six literal days of twenty-four hours each.

This seems to have become an absolute dogma with them. And, as is usually the case with religious dogmas, they cling to it so tenaciously that they are unable to see any other point of view.

They overlook the fact that five of these six 'days' of creation occurred before any man was on earth to experience them. Consequently, they need not necessarily have been days measured on a human timescale, but could very well have been days as God measures time. And that is a very different matter, since the Bible informs us that: 'A thousand years in thy [God's] sight are but as yesterday when it is past, or as a watch in the night,'[1] and: 'With the Lord one day is as a thousand years, and a thousand years as one day.'[2]

To most Bible readers those two passages are a plain warning that the days of creation might be anything but literal days of twenty-four hours. Not to the extreme literalist, however. He insists that our planet was only six days old when Adam was created, and is therefore only a few thousand years old now.

This leads him to a head-on collision with the professional geologists, who have compiled a vast amount of evidence that the earth is very many millions of years old, as we noted in chapter 2. Undaunted, the literalists reply that geologists are all barking up the wrong tree. The earth's geological features, they say, are really the result of Noah's Flood.

In recent years such a plausible case has been made out for this theory, which is known as Flood geology, that many Bible-believers have accepted it. Personally I think this is a tragedy, which in the long run can only do harm to the cause of Belief. As a Bible-believer I deem it an unnecessary theory, and as a scientist an incredible theory.

But we must not dismiss it without first taking a closer look at it.

Flood geology

There is nothing new about Flood geology. In the eighteenth century, when scientists and philosophers began to take a serious interest in the earth's crust, it was generally believed that fossils were the remains of creatures buried in the Flood. This was quite a reasonable assumption in view of the limited knowledge available in those days.

Nineteenth-century developments changed all that. Men like Cuvier and Lyell turned palaeontology and geology into systematic disciplines, and this produced a great advance in knowledge. As a result, masses of evidence accumulated which showed the earth to be very old, and that the Flood could not possibly account for the geological features of the earth's crust.

These new developments in geology, by the way, were not the consequence of evolutionary thinking. They took place in the first half of the nineteenth century, in the days before Darwin, when most scientists still believed in special creation.

The geologists' conclusions were so obviously sensible that they were almost universally accepted. Even the Bible-believing Christians of the late nineteenth century, with very few exceptions, agreed that the earth must be exceedingly old.

This happened because the nineteenth-century geologists were in such a strong position. If anyone demurred, they could take him into the countryside and point to the rock strata on which they based their findings, and say, 'See for yourself!' The kind of dissension and controversy which raged among biologists about evolution had no parallel in geology. The difference between the two sciences was reflected in the language used: men spoke (and still do) of the *theory* of evolution, but of the facts of geology.

For a hundred years the Flood theory of geology was as dead as the theory of phlogiston or the philosopher's stone. A brave attempt to revive it in the nineteen-twenties, by George McCready Price, was a flop.

Then in 1961 the totally unexpected happened. Two American professors, the civil engineer Dr Henry M. Morris and the theologian Dr John C. Whitcomb, published a 500-page book advocating a return to Flood geology.[3]

Needless to say, the book left professional geologists unmoved – or amused, or saddened, depending upon their religious convictions. Even the friendly geologist[4] who was persuaded by Morris and Whitcomb to write a foreword to their book said in it:

From the writer's viewpoint, as a professional geologist, these explanations and contentions [of Morris and Whitcomb] are difficult to accept. For the present at least ... I would prefer to hope that some other means of harmonisation of religion and geology, which

192

retains the essential structure of modern historical geology, could be found.

Yet, astonishingly, the book took a section of the religious world by storm. Many thousands of sincere Christians read it without really understanding it, and without spotting its numerous errors of fact and its many fallacious arguments.

Some of these have been pointed out in a long article[5] by a Christian geologist, Professor J. R. Van de Fliert of Amsterdam Free University, who himself confesses a 'belief in the Holy Scriptures as the reliable Word of God'.[6] Many of his objections to Flood geology are of too technical a character to reproduce here, but are well worth study by anyone wanting to go deeply into the subject.[7]

There is, however, one fatal objection to Flood geology which can be appreciated without any scientific knowledge, because it depends solely upon the evidence of our own eyes. Go for a walk along the sea coast, and notice how one beach is covered with white sand, another golden sand, another pebbles, and so on. These very different deposits have been neatly separated out by the action of the tides and the waves over a considerable period of time. Anyone can see that it is by slow, long-continued processes that water sorts things out.

But floods are a very different matter. *Floods mix things up*. If you have ever seen the aftermath of a flood, as I have, you will have been appalled by the chaos it has left behind. Mud, sand, stones, plants, trees, dead animals, man-made objects – all are mixed up together in hopeless confusion.

One look at an appropriate[8] cliff or quarry face is enough. The separate strata lie on top of each other like the layers of a sandwich cake. The divisions between them are cleancut and distinct.

All over the world the rock layers are separated in this way. The white cliffs of Dover are only a few miles from the black coal mines of Kent. In places the coal fields actually lie directly beneath the layers of chalk. But you won't find lumps of chalk in the coal seams, or bits of coal amidst the chalk.

Don't let us throw common sense out through the window. Floods always create turmoil – but the earth's crust is full of structure and order. It simply cannot have been fashioned by the greatest flood of all time.

The re-creation theory

This theory has rather more in its favour than the previous ones. It comes out of the literalist stable, but its exponents are nothing like as extreme in their literalism as the Flood geologists.

Their starting point is the same: the six days of creation are periods of twenty-four hours. But they respect the geological evidence that the earth is extremely old, and was inhabited by living things for many millions of years. This leaves them with the problem of reconciling a recent creation with an ancient earth. Their way out of this dilemma is as follows.

The first verse of the Bible says: 'In the beginning God created the heavens and the earth.' This, says the re-creationist, covers the *original* creation, which took place many million years ago. Following that first creation the earth was inhabited for millions of years by all sorts of creatures – perhaps including a race of man-like beings. The remains of many of these ancient living things form the fossils which pepper the earth's crust today.

Up to that point the re-creationsts are in complete accord with geologists. Then they suddenly part company. This first creation, says the re-creationist, came to a sticky end. Some unknown cataclysm wiped out every trace of life, and left the earth in the state described in the Bible's second verse, which they translate thus: 'The earth *became* [usual translation, *was*] without form and void, and darkness was upon the face of the deep.'

194

After that, says the re-creationist, God started all over again to create a new planet full of living things. This He did in six literal days, a few thousand years ago, as the remainder of Genesis chapter 1 describes.

It is difficult to rule out this theory completely. This might indeed be the sequence of events that Genesis 1 is describing. God might conceivably have wiped out a previous creation and replaced it by a new one.

Yet it does not seem very likely that this really happened. 'Without form and void' hardly seems a fitting description for a world full of well-preserved fossils, including complete dinosaur skeletons and frozen mammoths.

What is more, the geological record of life on this earth appears to be one long sequence. There is no geological evidence of a complete cut-off, followed by a fresh start a few thousand years ago.

It is, of course, possible that God deliberately removed all geological traces of the global catastrophe and the re-creation that followed. But there are no biblical grounds for thinking that He has, and it is difficult to imagine any reason why He should have done so.

All in all, the re-creation theory appears to leave too many unanswered questions for comfort.

Those 'days' of creation

We must be careful not to exaggerate the difficulty of reconciling Genesis with geology. Compared with all other ancient books, Genesis is superb. While his contemporaries were weaving tales about gods cutting each other in half, and making the heavens and earth out of the pieces and filling oceans with the blood, the writer of Genesis was quietly saying:

And God said, 'Let there be light'; and there was light. . . .
And God said, 'Let the waters under the heavens be

195

gathered together into one place, and let the dry land appear.' And it was so . . .
And God said, 'Let the earth put forth vegetation . . .'
And God said, 'Let the waters bring forth swarms of living creatures, and let birds fly above the earth . . .'
And God said, 'Let the earth bring forth living creatures according to their kinds . . .'
Then God said, 'Let us make man in our image . . .'[9]

Many thousands of scientists today find no difficulty in accepting that simple, dignified account of creation. If geologists were to make a short cine film of the earth's history, as seen though the eyes of an imaginary observer on earth, Genesis 1 would provide quite a good summary of the film. The only real problem is those six 'days'. What are we to make of them?

As we have already seen, it creates a whole load of difficulties to insist that they must be literal periods of twenty-four hours in which God actually did the work. And it is not necessary, since there are at least three other ways of understanding the 'days'.

The simplest solution is to assume that they merely stand for 'ages'. As we saw earlier, God says that a thousand years are to Him like a mere watch in the night, and so what He calls a day may really be an enormous period. There is nothing new about this conclusion. Augustine reached it in the fifth century from studying the text of Scripture alone, long before geologists found evidence that the earth is very old.[10]

A second possibility is that they are indeed literal days, but days of *revelation* instead of days of creation. Suppose that God spent six days showing Moses what creation had been like. In that case God could have compressed some three thousand million years of history into an experience of six days. What could be more natural than that Moses should have written up his experience in terms of the six days?[11]

A third alternative is that perhaps the 'days' were six

occasions on which God issued edicts, or statements of intent.[12] This possibility arises from the occurrence of the words, 'And God said, "Let such-and-such be",' which runs through Genesis 1 like a refrain. Other Bible books comment on this fact. For example:

> By the word of the Lord the heavens were made,
> And all their host by the breath of his mouth . . .
> For *he spoke*, and it came to be;
> *He commanded*, and it stood forth.[13]

Those verses remind us that immediately God ordains a thing, it is as good as accomplished; nothing can frustrate God's declared purpose. (That, says Paul, is why God could speak of Abraham's *future* children in the *past* tense.[14])

Now let us suppose that, before God began the actual physical work of creation, He spent six days explaining to His angels exactly what He was intending to do. If so, there would be a sense in which creation could be said to have taken place within those six days – because as soon as God had stated His intentions, the work was as good as done, even if it did take another few thousand million years to complete.

The Greek-speaking Jews of the days shortly before Christ may possibly have held this view. Their translation of Genesis 2:3 reads: 'And God blessed the seventh day and sanctified it, because in it he ceased from all his works which God *began* to do.'

With these three alternatives open to us, the six days do not present any real difficulty. We can still believe that Genesis is true, and also that the geologists are right about the long history of life on earth.

Successive creation

This opens the way to accepting the theory of successive creation. According to this view, God has been at work ever since the universe began, performing a great number of creative acts at intervals.

On this basis there is a very remarkable harmony between Genesis 1 and what the geologists have uncovered.

Originally the planet was a steamy, lifeless chaos, much as Venus is today. Then, as it cooled, clear air appeared between the clouds above and the seas beneath (Gen. 1:2–8).

Gradually, a great land mass rose up beneath the universal ocean (v. 9). Then vegetation appeared on the land (v. 11 and 12) and animal life came into being in the sea (vv. 20–2). The land animals followed (vv. 24 and 25) and last of all the first human pair appeared (vv. 26 and 27).

As I explained in some detail in *God's Truth*, it is possible to lump together most of the creatures which anthropologists regard as 'early man' as highly developed, but now extinct, forms of animal. In this way, Adam and Eve can be regarded as literal people, the first true human beings and the ancestors of the entire human race. If, as the anthropologist Victor Pearce has argued,[15] Adam was the first New Stone Age man, this would mean that he was created around 10,000 BC.

It is impossible to tell how many separate creative acts God has performed in the long history of our planet. But we can be certain that there were a great many, probably many millions of them. Sometimes they will have come singly, as with the creation of Adam, and sometimes in huge batches, as seems to have been the case in the 'Cambrian explosion' (see chapter 6).

Between these creative acts, and following them, a great deal of small-scale evolution is bound to have occurred – the sort of evolution that produced the Peppered moth in the nineteenth century, and insecticide-resistant mosquitoes and penicillin-resistant bacteria in the twentieth (see chapter 2).

This theory of successive creation, combined with the three alternative explanations of the six days mentioned above, is attractive to me for three reasons.

First and foremost, it seems to fit in with the teaching of both Genesis 1 and the remainder of the Bible quite well – just as well as any other theory proposed so far, in fact.

Secondly, it does what no other theory (either biblical or Darwinian) does: it accounts perfectly for all those gaps mentioned in chapter 6, which have baffled biologists and palaeontologists alike.

Finally, it is sufficiently close to the Darwinian theory to explain how so many biologists could have marched up the wrong road. One is reminded irresistibly of the situation illustrated in Figure 1, on page 34. The theory of the universe favoured by Dante was so nearly correct that we can only marvel at the brilliance of Ptolemy in formulating it. And yet it was terribly wrong. It needed one vital adjustment to put it right.

Darwinism, with its belief in large-scale, continuous evolution, is evidently like that, too. It needs only one vital adjustment to bring it into line with the theory that God created what Genesis calls the various 'kinds' of living things successively, over a vast period of time, while minor variations occurred naturally within all the 'kinds'.

It rather looks as if Darwin, like Ptolemy, was really not far from the truth – and yet terribly, terribly wrong.

NOTES

Chapter 1 (pages 11–17)
1. Ps. 19:1
2. Ps. 139:13, 14
3. Ps.14:1 and Ps. 53:1
4. Rom. 1:20
5. Acts 14:17
6. Acts 17:32. (See the whole context, especially verses 24–8.)
7. Isaac Asimov. Reprinted in his book, *Please Explain* (Abelard-Schumann, New York, 1975).
8. Isaac Newton, *Principia* (published in Latin, 1687; English translation by Motte).
9. H. McLachlan (ed), *Theological Manuscripts of Sir Isaac Newton* (University Press, Liverpool, 1950) 'A Short Scheme of True Religion', Section 2, 'Of Atheism'.
10. Julian Huxley, *Religion Without Revelation* (British Humanist Association, London, 1967) p. 58.
11. Albert Einstein, *The World as I See It* (Bodley Head, London, 1935) p. 5.
12. Quoted in *The Observer*, London, 1 Aug. 1976.
13. According to John Young, *The Case Against Christ* (Falcon, London, 1971) p. 29.
14. I. Breach, 'Scientists who believe in God', *New Scientist*, 26 May 1977, p. 478.
15. Likewise, even though I once published a paper expounding the advantages of sticking strictly to SI units in mathematical work, I shall in this book keep to such familiar units as pounds, miles and gallons.

Chapter 2 (pages 18–35)
1. *New Scientist*, Oct. 1975, p. 110.
2. A great many philosophers, scientists and historians broadly agree with this simple analysis. They see this as the central issue, upon which everything else depends. See, for example, p. 101 and p. 121 of the paperback edition of *The Existence of God* (Cornell University Press, New York, 1965) by Wallace I. Matson, an agnostic professor of philosophy; also the beginning of chapter 2 of *Chance and Necessity* (Collins, London, 1972) by Jacques Monod.
3. *Sunday Times*, London, 13 Oct. 1974, p. 3.

4. *Nature, 245* (1973).
5. John C. Whitcomb, *The Early Earth* (Baker Book House, Grand Rapids, Mich. 1972) p. 132.
6. 'At Random', a TV programme screened on 21 Nov. 1959, reported in S. Tax, *Evolution After Darwin* (University Press, Chicago, 1960) Vol. 3, pp. 41–65.
7. A. Hardy, *The Biology of God* (Cape, London, 1975) p. 24.
8. *Nature, 239* (1972) p. 420.
9. Sir Karl Popper is a professor of the philosophy of science, who has been largely responsible for the more humble spirit shown by many scientists nowadays. A scientist is described as 'Popperian' (a term of high praise) if he admits that he does not know all the answers, that his views are only tentative, and that he is always ready to modify or abandon those views if further work by himself or some other scientist shows this to be necessary.
10. L. C. Birch and P. R. Ehrlich, *Nature, 214* (1967) pp. 349–52.
11. Opinions differ as to whether Darwin was really a genius. It is sometimes argued that all he did was to take up the thoughts of a number of his contemporaries who were also talking of evolution and arrange these in a systematic way, along with a great deal of evidence gleaned from his own observations, so as to produce a convincing case. I personally see no reason why we should not at least give him the benefit of the doubt, however.
12. There is a fairly common belief in some Christian circles that all the sedimentary rocks are about this age, and were deposited during the Flood. For evidence that this cannot possibly be so, see the Appendix.
13. There is not room here to discuss the impact of geology upon the early chapters of Genesis. I have dealt with that in chapters 21 to 23 of *God's Truth* (Marshall Morgan & Scott, London, 1973; revised paperback edition by Lakeland, London, 1977).
14. B. V. Derjaguin and N. V. Churaev, 'Nature of Anomalous Water', *Nature, 244* (1973) p. 430.
15. Isaac Asimov, *Guide to Science* (Pelican, London, 1975) Vol. 1, p. 111.
16. C. S. Lewis, *The Discarded Image* (University Press, Cambridge, 1964) chapter 5.

Chapter 3 (pages 36–52)
1. *Glasgow Herald*, 12 Oct. 1972.
2. This raises the highly difficult question: what do we mean by facts? Philosophers would probably refrain from using the word at all in such a context, on the ground that there are no

such things as facts, but only statements of differing degrees of probability. My definition of a fact is a statement that is very well supported by solid evidence. Since this definition provokes more questions of logic than it resolves it will certainly not satisfy a philosopher, but it is probably quite good enough for the purposes of this book.

3. Jacques Monod, *Chance and Necessity* (Collins, London, 1972).

4. The opening paragraph of chapter 2.

5. John Lewis, *Beyond Chance and Necessity* (Garnstone Press, London, 1974).

6. John Maynard Smith, *Nature, 252* (1974) p. 762.

7. Ernst Chain, *Social Responsibility and the Scientist in Modern Western Society* (Council of Christians and Jews, London, 1970).

8. Op. cit. (Fontana edition) p. 33.

9. Op. cit., p. 25.

10. Op. cit., pp. 30, 31.

11. 'Teleological' is a word used by philosophers to describe the argument which says that everything in nature is so cleverly designed that it must have been created by a great Designer, to serve some purpose. They make a clear distinction between this and a second kind of argument which they call 'cosmological'; this is the argument that says every effect has a cause, and if you follow the chain of cause and effect back to its beginning you have to conclude that the universe was created by some great First Cause. Although I have avoided using these terms, my first point in chapter 2 is really a combination of these two arguments, expressed in non-technical language.

12. Op. cit., pp. 25, 26.

13. *Nature, 239* (1972) p. 420.

14. The International Series of Monographs in Pure and Applied Biology – Zoology Division (Pergamon Press, Oxford).

15. G. A. Kerkut, *Implications of Evolution* (Pergamon Press, Oxford, 1960. Reprinted 1973).

16. Theodosius Dobzhansky, *Genetics and the Origin of Species* (Columbia University Press, 2nd edn., 1941) p. 8.

17. *Nature, 238* (1972) p. 116.

18. The Everyman Library (Dent, London, 1956).

19. 'The human understanding is of its own nature prone to suppose the existence of more order and regularity in the world than it finds, And though there be many things which are singular and unmatched, yet it devises for them parallels and conjugates and relatives which do not exist. Hence the fiction that all celestial bodies move in perfect circles' (*Novum*

Organum, I, 45). Cited by C. S. Lewis, *Miracles* (Fontana, London, 1960) p. 31.

20. Ian Roxburgh, 'Is Special Relativity Right or Wrong', *New Scientist*, 28 Sept. 1972, p. 602.
21. Peter Medawar, *Reith Lectures – The Future of Man* (Methuen, London, 1960) p. 62.
22. Julian Huxley, *Evolution, the Modern Synthesis* (Allen & Unwin, London, 1942) p. 473.
23. E. G. Conklin, *Man Real and Ideal* (Scribner, New York, 1943) p. 147.
24. Julian Huxley (ed.), *The Humanist Frame* (Allen & Unwin, London, 3rd imp., 1965).
25. Alister Hardy, *The Biology of God* (Jonathan Cape, London, 1975) p. 208.
26. C. H. Waddington, 'Towards a Theoretical Biology', *Nature*, *218* (1968) p. 527.
27. Tomoko Ohta, 'Mutational Pressure as the Main Cause of Molecular Evolution and Polymorphism', *Nature*, *252* (1974) p. 351.
28. R. A. Crowson, 'Anti-Darwinism Among the Molecular Biologists', *Nature*, *254* (1975) p. 464.
29. Nigel Calder, 'Evolving Evolution,' *Nature*, *255* (1975) p. 8.

Chapter 4 (pages 53–70)

1. According to John Gribbin, *Nature*, *259* (1976) p. 15.
2. See R. E. D. Clark, *The Universe: Plan or Accident?* (Paternoster, London, 1949) pp. 14–17.
3. Perhaps I should put it on record that the frequently repeated word 'luck' in this chapter means, 'luck, as an atheist would describe it, or a blessing from the Creator as I regard it myself'.
4. This is not solely a matter of distance from the sun; the long period of rotation and the 'greenhouse effect' of the Venusian atmosphere also play an important part. But even without these additional effects Venus probably would still be too hot to accommodate life easily.
5. Isaac Asimov, *Guide to Science* Vol. 2, p. 116.
6. W. S. Broecker, 'A Kinetic Model for the Chemical Composition of Sea Water', *Quaternary Research*, *1* (1971) p. 188.
7. F. J. Dyson, 'Energy in the Universe', *Scientific American*, *224* (Sept. 1971) p. 50.
8. David Foster, *The Intelligent Universe* (Abelard-Schuman, London, 1975).
9. *New Scientist*, 6 Feb. 1975, p. 304.
10. The atheists' stock answer to this is that the universe also is (literally) 'astronomical' in size, and consequently the fantasti-

cally unlikely conditions required for the existence of life were bound to occur somewhere. There is a fallacy in this argument – see the section entitled, 'The way chance works', in chapter 5.

Chapter 5 (pages 71–85)

1. John Young, *The Case Against Christ*, p. 36.
2. Isaac Asimov, *Please Explain*.
3. Ibid.
4. *Chance and Necessity*, p. 134.
5. G. Cairns-Smith, 'Genes Made of Clay', *New Scientist*, 24 Oct. 1974, p. 274.
6. John Maynard Smith, *The Theory of Evolution* (Pelican, London, 3rd edn., 1975) p. 102; this admission occurs in a chapter newly written for this edition, on 'The Origin and Early Evolution of Life'.
7. To calculate the odds, all you need to do is to multiply 6 by itself a hundred times. With the aid of a table of logarithms, this can be shown to produce a number greater than 10^{77} (one followed by 77 noughts).
8. For example, James F. Coppedge, in *Evolution: Possible or Impossible?* (Zondervan, Grand Rapids, Mich., 1973).
9. I have oversimplified here. The experiments are really rather complicated and involve mixtures of gaseous chemicals as well as liquids and, in some cases, solids also.
10. An enzyme is a protein with the ability to act as a specific catalyst. This means that each enzyme will normally cause one particular chemical reaction to occur, and no other. An enzyme can therefore be regarded as a miniature chemical factory, capable of manufacturing just one chemical product, provided that the necessary raw materials are available. (But see following note.)
11. This is broadly true but not absolutely so. Some exceptional enzymes can promote two or more different reactions. These exceptions to the general rule, however, are not numerous enough or important enough to affect the argument of this chapter.
12. For example: M. Calvin, *Chemical Evolution* (Oxford University Press, London, 1969); S. L. Miller and L. E. Orgel, *The Origins of Life on the Earth* (Prentice-Hall, Hemel Hempstead, 1974).
13. *The Origins of Life on the Earth*.
14. M. Dixon and E. Webb, *Enzymes* (Longmans, London 2nd edn., 1964) p. 699.
15. The odds against two improbable events happening together

at random are obtained by multiplying the two separate pro-babilities. For example, if the chances against the nucleic acid being formed are, shall we say, a thousand to one (this is a huge underestimate, but it will do to illustrate the principle involved), and the odds against the necessary enzymes being formed nearby are a million to one, then the odds against them both being formed together are a thousand million to one. This is a basic principle of mathematics, and is as inescapable as the multiplication table. F. B. Salisbury (*Nature, 224* (1969) p. 342) attempted to calculate the actual odds against similar dual events occurring in the course of evolution, and concluded that these were of the order of ten to the power of several hundred! (That is, a one, followed by several hundred noughts.) So far as I have been able to ascertain, his arguments have never been faulted.

16. Op. cit., p. 135.
17. A. I. Oparin, *The Origin of Life* (published in Russian in 1924, English translation published by Oliver & Boyd, Edinburgh, 1936)

Chapter 6 (pages 86–102)
1. J. M. Smith, *The Theory of Evolution* (Penguin, London, 3rd edn., 1975) p. 287.
2. C. J. O. Harrison, 'Feathering and flight evolution in *Archaeopteryx*', *Nature, 263* (1976) p. 762.

3. For example, J. M. Smith, *The Theory of Evolution*.
4. Such as J. H. Ostrum, in *Quarterly Review of Biology, 49* (1974) p. 27.
5. J. A. Clark and J. Cena, 'Plants, Animals and Energy', *Physics Bulletin, 27* (1976) p. 548.
6. V. B. Wigglesworth, 'Evolution of insect wings and flight', *Nature, 246* (1973) p. 127.
7. Reported in *New Scientist*, 13 Dec. 1973, p. 752.
8. K. Schmidt-Nielsen, 'The physiology of the camel', *American Scientist*, Dec. 1959, p. 140.
9. R. A. McCance *et al*. Proc. Roy. Soc. B, *185* (1974) p. 263.
10. H. J. Frith (ed.), *Complete Book of Australian Birds* (Reader's Digest Services, Sydney) pp. 136–7.
11. J. M. Smith, op. cit., p. 197.
12. J. Krebs, 'Sexual selection and the handicap principle', *Nature, 261* (1976) p. 192.
13. Ps. 104:24 (GNB)
14. S. Stanley, 'Cropping and the Cambrian explosion', *New Scientist*, 17 Jan. 1974, p. 131.
15. R. B. Goldschmidt, *The Material Basis of Evolution* (University Press, Yale, 1940).

16. J. L. Brown, *The Evolution of Behaviour* (Norton, New York, 1975).

17. *Nature, 259* (1976) p. 427.

18. T. N. George, 'Fossils in evolutionary perspective,' *Science Progress*, Jan. 1960, p. 1.

19. G. G. Simpson, *The Major Features of Evolution* (Columbia University Press, New York, 1953) p. 360.

20. Readers seeking further details of these gaps in the fossil record will find hundreds of them listed by Douglas Dewar in *The Transformist Illusion* (Dehoff Publications, Murfreesboro, Tennessee, 1957), a devastating scholarly exposure of the weaknesses of Darwinism which has never been adequately answered.

21. J. P. A. Angseesing, 'The burden of proof', *Nature, 242* (1973) p. 214.

Chapter 7 (pages 103–14)

1. For the sake of simplicity I am ignoring the profoundly important difference between prokaryotes and eukaryotes, which is not essential to the argument here. Those who appreciate the difference will recognise another of those huge leaps that are so baffling to evolutionists. The wild guesses offered as explanations of the origin of eukaryotes – such as, 'symbiotic union of several simple prokaryotic organisms, which subsequently merged to form one complex cell' – are a good illustration of the way many evolutionists brush aside huge difficulties. It seems as if in evolutionary theory, provided you can guess a possible solution to a problem, it does not matter how wildly improbable your guess is – you are still entitled to claim that the problem is tentatively solved. It is no wonder that most evolutionists sound so confident; when you play a game with rules like that you can't lose. This sort of behaviour by his colleagues led no less a biologist than W. R. Thompson (cf. chap. 3 note 18) to describe evolutionary thinking as 'fragile towers of hypotheses based on hypotheses, where fact and fiction mingle in an inextricable confusion.'

2. For an up-to-date survey of knowledge (or the lack of it!) on this question, see J. M. Thoday, 'Non-Darwinian evolution and biological progress', *Nature, 255* (1975) p. 675.

3. H. Schildknecht, 'Evolutionary peaks in the defensive chemistry of insects', *Endeavour, 30* (Sept. 1971) p. 136.

4. Described by J. Dahl in an article in the German weekly, *Die Zeit*, 9 Aug. 1974. English translation, 'The Sawfly Defies All Evolutionary Logic', in *The Plain Truth*, Sept.–Oct. 1976, p. 16.

5. I am indebted for this example to Norman Macbeth, whose

Darwin Retried (Gambit, Boston, 1971) is a mine of information on the weaknesses of Darwinism.

6. Not a family in the strict biological sense, but a phylum; it includes creatures as diverse as corals, sea-anemones and jellyfish.

7. A summary in *New Scientist,* 14 April 1977, p. 75, of a paper by M. and B. Robinson in the Spring 1977 number of the *Smithsonian Institute Research Reports.*

8. Ibid.

9. M. T. Ghiselin, *The Economy of Nature and the Evolution of Sex* (University of California Press, Berkeley and London, December 1974).

10. *Nature,* 254 (1975) p. 221.

11. G. C. Williams, *Sex and Evolution* (Princeton University Press, Princeton, 1975).

12. *Nature,* 258 (1975), p. 32.

13. Cited by Macbeth, op. cit., p. 101.

14. Cited by R. E. D. Clark, *Darwin, Before and After* (Paternoster Press, London, 1948) p. 93.

15. It is evident from the way he uses the word that 'Panglossianism' is to Maynard Smith practically a synonym for 'teleology'. This is not the usual literary meaning of the word, which is derived from Voltaire's over-optimistic character, Dr Pangloss. Science frequently takes hold of an ordinary word with a broad meaning and gives it a narrow, specialised meaning, as biologists appear to have done with this word.

Chapter 8 (pages 115–31)

1. Gen. 1:27

2. C. E. Oxnard, 'The place of the australopithecines in human evolution: grounds for doubt?', *Nature,* 258 (1975) p. 389.

3. S. L. Washburn and C. S. Lancaster, in *Man the Hunter* (ed. by R. B. Lee and R. Devore, Aldine Pub. Co., Chicago, 1968) p. 296.

4. In this sort of situation most or all of the gene pool would be destroyed, so that kin selection would not operate. *Homo sapiens* appears to be the only species addicted to the large-scale and systematic destruction of his own kind; it is remarkable that evolutionary anthropologists should so largely ignore the probable effect of this unique characteristic of our species on the course of natural selection.

5. R. J. Andrew, *Nature,* 236 (1972) p. 292.

6. A. Montagu, *Man: His First Two Million Years* (Columbia University Press, New York, 1969) p. 125 – cited by W. Frair

and P. W. Davis, *The Case for Creation* (Moody, Chicago, 1972 edn.) p. 15.

7. L. Eiseley, *Darwin's Century* (Doubleday, Toronto, 1961) pp. 310–14, and *The Immense Journey* (Vintage Books, London, 1958) pp. 84–5. Cited by Macbeth, op. cit., p. 103.
8. The menopause is not similar to the cessation of oestrus in the lower mammals. Oestrus can cease at a relatively early age if the animal concerned is ill or under stress. But it can just as easily continue into old age if the animal's circumstances are favourable. The inevitable cut-off in a healthy woman's reproductive life while she is still in her prime has no counterpart in any other species.
9. Richard Dawkins, *The Selfish Gene* (Oxford University Press, London, 1976) p. 135.
10. *New Scientist*, 4 Sept. 1975, p. 523.
11. Cited by Eric Ashby, *Nature 255* (1975) p. 747.
12. R. Roberts, *Is There a God?* (Walker, Bristol, 1931) p. 25. (Articles reprinted from *Good Company*.)
13. 1 Cor. 7:4.
14. R. Targ and H. Puthoff, 'Information transmission under conditions of sensory screening', *Nature, 251* (1974) p. 602.

Chapter 9 (pages 132–47)

1. Two examples from among many are Job 3:11–23 and Ps. 74:1.
2. See, for instance the opening remarks by the unbeliever Wallace Matson in the section, 'Part III – Evil', in *The Existence of God*.
3. C. S. Lewis, *The Problem of Pain* (Bles, London, 1940) p. 16.
4. For a useful collection of quotations on this subject, see J. W. Wenham. *The Goodness of God* (Inter-Varsity Press, London, 1974) pp. 199–204.
5. Isaac Asimov, *Words of Science* (Harrap, London, 1974). (Article, 'Ecology'.)
6. 2 Sam. 1:26; Luke 7:37–50; John 15:13.
7. There are other aspects of this subject which there is no space to discuss here, especially the relationship between free will and eternal life. I have dealt with this at some length in chapter 24 of *God's Truth*.
8. Rom. 7:13–25 is an outstanding example of this.
9. Gen. 1:27; Ps. 8:5; Heb. 2:7.
10. I was sorely tempted to introduce the slick Latinism 'penangelus' here. But 'near-angel' says the same thing much more intelligibly and so it will have to serve, despite its clumsiness.
11. It is rather a pity that some Christian writers on the philosophy of science and religion – for example, Donald

Mackay in *The Clockwork Image* (Inter-Varsity Press, London 1974) pp. 13–15 – categorically deny that there could be any connection between the indeterminacy of quantum processes and the indeterminacy of mental processes. They may turn out to be right, in the end. Yet, in view of the enormous number of information 'bits' that can be stored and processed in a relatively small mass of active brain cells, it is conceivable that some mental processes might involve energy transfers sufficiently close to the quantum level for statistical determinacy not to apply. Although at present it is not possible to postulate a mechanism by which this could occur, it is not unreasonable to suppose that quantum-indeterminacy might possibly lead to thought-indeterminacy. To deny this possibility is to assume knowledge that we do not possess.

12. J. B. S. Haldane, *Possible Worlds* (William Heinemann, London, 1940).

13. C. T. Gorham, *The Gospel of Rationalism* (Thinker's Library, London, 1942) p. 59.

Chapter 10 (pages 148–59)

1. In *Mere Christianity* (Fontana edn., London, 1955) chapter 1. The first five chapters of this book contain one of the most convincing and clearly presented arguments for the existence of God ever written.

2. According to various allegations by Amnesty International.

3. The Christian view, of course, is that this training can only be with the aid of divine revelation: that is why God has given us a Bible.

4. Surprising though it may seem, some Christians will probably be reluctant to accept this statement that there is an absolute standard of right and wrong. As a matter of fact, there have long been two views on the matter. One view is that certain things are right in themselves, and that that is why God commands them. The other view is that God can command anything He likes, and whatever He commands then becomes right: for instance, so long as He commands us to be honest, then honesty remains right; but if He should ever order us to cheat one another, then dishonesty would become right. For a brief summary of the background to the two views, see C. S. Lewis, *The Problem of Pain*, chapter 6.

As with many theological controversies, there is some truth on both sides. The second view is certainly true of some secondary issues, such as the offering of animal sacrifices and ritual circumcision, and I personally believe (though these are more controversial matters) that it is true of keeping the Sabbath and making war, also. But the Bible evidently teaches (read Rom. 13:8–10 along with 1 John 4:8) that the first view is true of the really fundamental moral principles, which seem to be embedded in God's very nature, so to speak. This probably explains why mankind has always been in practically unanimous agreement about the fundamental issues of morality, while differing widely about matters of detail.

5. C. H. Waddington, *The Ethical Animal* (Allen & Unwin, London, 1960).
6. The most notable of these is probably E. O. Wilson, whose *Sociobiology* (Harvard Bellknap, Cambridge, Mass., 1975) raised a storm of controversy among biologists.
7. H. G. Wells, *When the Sleeper Wakes* (Sphere Books, London, 1967) chapter 19.
8. *Philosophical Essays* (Allen & Unwin, London, 1966) p. 24.

Chapter 11 (pages 160–70)
1. My own attempt to provide such an answer is *God's Truth*, which, although written first, can be regarded as a sequel to this book.
2. An invaluable source-book, with reference to hundreds of other useful books on Christian evidence, is J. McDowell, *Evidence That Demands a Verdict* (Campus Crusade for Christ International, San Bernardino, California, 1972).
3. Dan. 4:25
4. Isa. 43:1, 9, 10
5. Amos 3:7
6. Deut. 18:22
7. Deut. 28:37, 63–5
8. Jer. 46:28
9. Jer. 31:10, 11
10. H. Wouk, *This is My God* (Revised edn., Collins, London, 1973) chapter 22.
11. Ezek. 36:22–31
12. Deut. 32:8 (English Revised Version)
13. In particular the study groups of the Food and Agriculture Organisation of the United Nations have provided much useful, though terrifying, information.

Chapter 12 (pages 171–86)
1. Cited by W. Sears, *Thief in the Night* (George Ronald, Oxford, 1976) p. 232.
2. Ibid., p. 231.
3. K. Tait, *My Father Bertrand Russell* (Gollancz, London, 1976).
4. Gal. 5:22, 23
5. John 6:63
6. This statement, which oversimplifies a complex subject, would

be indignantly repudiated by many Buddhists. Nirvana, which Gautama is said to have attained, is not exactly a state of non-existence. However, for the practical purpose of my argument the subtle difference between entering Nirvana and ceasing to exist is of no consequence.

7. Matt. 16:16
8. John 20:28
9. John 10:20
10. Mark 3:22, and elsewhere.
11. John 10:33, and elsewhere.
12. John 10:36
13. John 10:30
14. John 8:29
15. John 8:46
16. John 10:17, 18
17. Mark 9:31
18. Matt. 26:28
19. John 16:28
20. Matt. 26:64
21. Matt. 25:31, 32
22. John 5:26–9
23. For a simple presentation by an eminent scholar of the evidence as it stood a few years ago, see F. F. Bruce, *The New Testament Documents* (Inter-Varsity Press, London, 1960). The case for a very early date for the four Gospels is now so powerful that even such an extreme modernist as the former Bishop of Woolwich, J. A. T. Robinson, of *Honest to God* fame, has argued in favour of it in *Redating the New Testament* (SCM Press, London, 1976).
24. Acts 1:3
25. John 20:11–18
26. Luke 24:13–31
27. Luke 24:36–43
28. Luke 24:27; Acts 1:3
29. The story of Nicodemus in John 3 is a case in point.
30. Saul of Tarsus was doubtless in this category. See Gal. 1:13, 14.
31. Matt. 23:1–28; John 2:13–16
32. Rev. 3:20
33. Rom. 10:17
34. Matt. 7:7, 8

Appendix
1. Ps. 90:4
2. 2 Pet. 3:8

3. H. M. Morris and J. C. Whitcomb. *The Genesis Flood* (Evangelical Press, St Albans, 1969).

4. Prof. J. C. McCampbell of the University of Southwestern Louisiana.

5. J. R. Van de Fliert, 'Fundamentalism and the Fundamentals of Geology', *Journal of the American Scientific Affiliation, 21* (3) Sept. 1969. Reprinted in England in *Faith and Thought, 98* (1) Autumn 1970, pp. 11–42.

6. Ibid., 4th paragraph. (It is only fair to say that his view of the Bible is rather more liberal than that of most Bible-believing Christians.)

7. See also J. Byrt, 'The roles of the Bible and of science in understanding creation', *Faith and Thought, 103* (3) 1976, p. 158.

8. By 'appropriate' I mean one revealing several strata of sedimentary or metamorphic rocks, or sedimentary rocks with igneous intrusions.

9. Gen. 1:3–26

10. See p. 37 of note 15, below.

11. This idea is thought to have been originated by a German, J. H. Kurtz, in the nineteenth century. It has been worked out in great detail by P. J. Wiseman in *Clues to Creation in Genesis* (Marshall, Morgan & Scott, London, rev. edn., 1977). Robert E. D. Clark has also reasoned strongly in its favour in *The Christian Stake in Science* (Paternoster Press, Exeter, 1967) chapter 16.

12. I am indebted for this suggestion, as I am for a great many other things, to my friend Peter Watkins.

13. Ps. 33:6, 9

14. Rom. 4:17

15. E. K. V. Pearce, *Who Was Adam?* (Paternoster Press, Exeter, 1969).

INDEX OF AUTHORS

GENERAL INDEX

Recent Marshalls Paperbacks

MY ROUGH DIAMOND

Doris Lemon with Anne Tyler

'Not all women have husbands who turn out to be viciously tempered, drunkards, or even convicts—but some women do. It can be a nightmare to be married to such a man: the isolation of it, the shame, the loneliness you feel. And fear! Fear for yourself, for the children. How do you cope? Where do you get the stamina and endurance from?

I've written this book so as to share with you my experiences—and the lessons I learned from them—and to tell you that God is able to make all the difference.

Of course, it was marvellous when Fred became a Christian. It was the start of a whole new life for us. But maybe your husband isn't a Christian, and you're all alone and fed up. That's how it was for me for many years. Here's the lessons I learned from my marriage, and not only how I learned to live with, but also, how to help my rough diamond . . .'

Doris has been married to her husband, Fred, for twenty-seven years. Fred Lemon's story is told in *Breakout*, and he has also written *Going Straight* and *Breakthrough*.

FREED FOR LIFE

Rita Nightingale

'Today, at round 11 am I got a twenty-year prison sentence. It didn't come as a shock, but it certainly came as a surprise. I was expecting over thirty . . .'

Prison Diary, 9 December 1977

Rita's sentence in Bangkok for drug-smuggling caused world-wide headlines. But the **real** story is how she became a Christian whilst in a Thai prison and how her life was transformed.

BETRAYED

Stan Telchin

Betrayed! That was the stunned reaction of Stan Telchin, a successful Jewish businessman, when his daughter Judy rang him up to say that she had accepted Jesus as her Messiah.

Stan was shocked by Judy's new commitment, regarding it as a betrayal of their family, their race, their heritage. Grimly, he decided to prove to Judy how wrong she was, and so re-unite the family. He began an angry quest which went on for weeks, then months. In searching through the Bible he not only came to understand what it meant to be a Christian, but what it really meant to be a Jew, and, finally, what Jesus Christ means to all men and women. At the end of his quest, he finds that the rest of his family have all been on the same path . . .

This true story rings with the excitement of prophecy fulfilled in our day. It is full of fascinating insights into how Jesus was regarded by the Jews of his time, and how they see Him now. It is about a whole family's search for true faith and the healing of seemingly irreparable division.

WITH GOD MY HELPER

Ruth Sanford

A Christian woman shouldn't be satisfied with simply 'getting through' her day.

God wants you to do more than just survive—he planned your life to be rich and rewarding. He wants you to have victory over your daily struggles, and he wants you to be respected and honoured.

Many women believe this truth, but don't know how to make it a reality in their lives. Ruth Sanford shares how women can overcome common personal problems such as anxiety, guilt, discouragement, bitterness, and a poor self-image, to experience the full joy and contentment of being a Christian woman.

ORDER! ORDER!
Ramon Hunston

A scene in Parliament today. The Speaker, resplendent in his robes, subdues the unruly backbenchers . . . 'Order! Order!'

George Thomas now holds one of the highest posts in the land. His rise from the childhood poverty of the Welsh mining valleys, living with four brothers and sisters in a tiny Rhondda 'underhouse', is a remarkable testimony to his character, determination, and above all to his Christian faith. He explains to Ramon Hunston how it has weathered both the storms of doubt and the pressures of holding down one of the most demanding jobs which can be imagined. He relates it to his socialist commitment and his actions and attitudes in public life. As he says of himself—'It is amazing what God can do with a lad from the Rhondda with a patch on his trousers.'

FROM PRISON TO PULPIT
Vic Jackopson

'Father died when he was a year old.
Mother deserted.
Family broken up.
Failed fostering experiment.
Above average intelligence.
One more chance.'

Vic was used to probation officers pleading his case in court. He had learnt to take care of himself early on in the orphanage, but years of fighting, stealing and burgling had brought him to the end of the line.

'God, if you are there, you've got ten days to change my life and if you haven't done it by then you've copped it.'

Vic prayed, God acted. It wasn't always easy from then on, but living by the grace of God rather than by his own fists Vic found a new inner strength and security. Instead of taking from others he now teaches and lives the new life Christ brings into the hearts of men and women.